S0-BAK-719

Sitanka

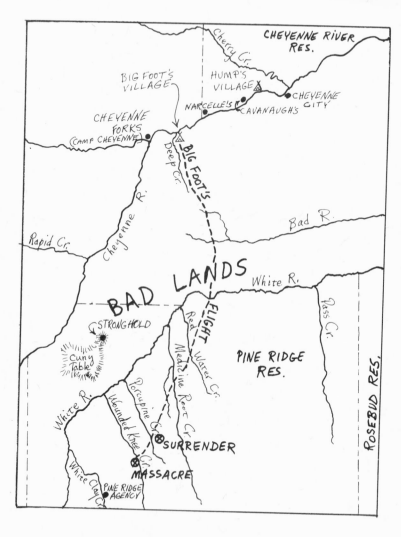

The trail to Wounded Knee.

SITANKA

The Full Story of Wounded Knee

By

FORREST W. SEYMOUR

THE CHRISTOPHER PUBLISHING HOUSE
W. HANOVER, MASSACHUSETTS 02339

Printed in
The United States of America

This is an account of the major events preceding, during, and immediately after the battle of 1890 at Wounded Knee—not altogether as the United States Army records tell it, and not altogether as the aggrieved Indian survivors remembered it a half century later, but reconstructed as truthfully in main outline as it can be pieced together from both these sources and numerous others cited in the Acknowledgments at the end of this book, especially that vast store of personal interviews with Wounded Knee participants by Judge Eli S. Ricker which are now in the custody of the Nebraska State Historical Society.

CHAPTER I

THE SAVIOR

Alongside the narrow, blacktop road which meanders southwest from Kadoka, a carefully painted yellow and black sign announces, "You Are Entering the Land of Red Cloud—Pine Ridge Indian Reservation—Home of Oglala Sioux Indian Tribe."

The Dakotas have long since accepted the label Sioux, although in the beginning they resented it—and for good reason. It was given to them by the Ojibwas, their deadly enemies for more than 200 years. The Ojibwas, or Chippewas, had called them *Nadowessi*, "Snake-like" or "Hated Enemy." The French trappers added their own pluralization, making it *Nadowessioux*, and then promptly dropped everything except the final syllable. So the name originally had come from the detested Algonquian language, rather than the Dakotan or what we now call Siouan, and in addition it derived from a hateful epithet.

The French fur hunters came down the St. Lawrence River into the Great Lakes region in the 17th century when the Ojibwas, having acquired firearms from the French, were driving the last of the Dakotas ahead of them into the northern Great Plains. Then, in the 18th century, the fur traders moved on westward and made friends with the Dakotas, also.

These Frenchmen were not only honest traders, on the whole, but when they took Indian women into their lodges they considered them wives. The Frenchmen's squaws raised children and their fathers were proud of them. The trappers taught their women something about

9

cleanliness and sanitation, how to get their food up off the ground and cook it properly, how to make efficient gardens and treat common illnesses. By the early 19th century there were French names all over the territory— part-Indian interpreters and scouts and freighters and buffalo-hunters.

The French traders also gave several of the Teton Dakota bands their modern names. In 1763 one branch of the family had got caught in a terrible prairie fire, and the legs and backsides of many survivors were badly scarred from their burns. The Dakotas thereafter called them *Sicangu,* or Burned Thighs, which the French reduced to Brulés or Burned Ones. In a similar way, the *Itazipoo* band had been so named by their kinsmen because they were once caught by an enemy without their bows and arrows, and were all but wiped out. The French translated the Siouan name "Without Bows" as Sans Arc, and that is the name commonly used to this day.

The Dakota nation had two divisions when the white man's civilization began to overtake the tribe. The eastern branch, or Santees, were settled mainly in the lush grass prairies and woods of Minnesota. By the time of the Civil War they were tired of being crowded, cheated and abused by the flood of white settlers, and they staged a widespread uprising which killed scores of pioneer families. But their killing spree merely turned legions of white soldiers loose on them in devastating retribution, and thereafter the four Santee bands of Mdewkantons, Wahpekutes, Sissetons and Wahpetons were docile and helpless on their little reservations, awaiting their handouts from the government like American Indians everywhere.

But while this struggle of the Santees was going on, the western branches of Dakotas were just beginning to be hurt badly by the white invasion. The Yanktons were finally pushed out of northwestern Iowa, the Yanktonais out of eastern Dakota Territory, and they naturally fled across the Missouri River to their cousins, the Tetons. The area west of the Missouri River was semi-arid or worse, but for this very reason the great buffalo herds wintered here where they could get through the light snow easily to the prairie grass beneath. Since the Teton Dakotas lived on the buffalo for their food, clothing, and much of their shelter, the region was reasonably hospitable to them. In the next couple of decades, as the buffalo herds were destroyed by the white man and the Dakotas were forced out of their mountain hunting preserves farther west, the Missouri River country would become a place of desolation for them.

The greatest tribe of the western Dakotas was the Tetons. They did not pronounce the name of their nation with a "D" as the eastern branch, or Santees, did. They called themselves *Lakota*. But the white man had come upon the Santees first, so all of the federation was doomed to be labelled Dakotas. (The Yanktons had pronounced it still differently: *Nakota*.)

The name, however pronounced, means "friends" or "allies." And the tribal name of Teton is a contraction of the Siouan phrase (*Tentah Ahtunwan*) for "Prairie Villagers," distinguishing these plains Indians from the Santee tribe on the long grass farther east.

Driven westward in the 17th and 18th centuries by the pressures arising from white immigration along the Great Lakes, the Dakotas took to the wild horses emerging from the Spanish Southwest and became expert horsemen, buffalo hunters and fighters. Because they followed the buffalo herds a good part of the year, their culture was predominantly nomadic.

The homeland of the Tetons had become, by the second quarter of the 19th century, the whole range from the Platte River northward through Dakota and Wyoming to southern Montana; and from the Missouri River on the east to the Yellowstone country of the Rocky Mountains on the west—the Powder River highlands and the Big Horn Mountains being their cherished hunting preserves, and the Black Hills of Dakota their most holy place and sacred rendezvous.

The bands within the Teton tribe were these: Oglala (the largest), Brulé, Hunkpapa, Minneconjou, Two Kettle (Oohenonpa), Sans Arc, the Blackfeet Sioux (Sihasapa). Although not as numerous as the Oglalas, the Brulés were equally respected because of their ferocity and untamed spirit.

In the year 1889 when this story begins, many of the Indians on the Dakota reservations had been there for nearly twenty years, but their living space had been sharply reduced several times in that period. Most of them, however, had only come in submissively following the battles along the Little Big Horn and elsewhere in 1876-77. And a few bands had run to Canada at that time to preserve their freedom, returning to the reservations only in 1881, so these latter had suffered reservation life now for a mere eight years or so.

But to all of them, the new imprisonment was frustrating and galling, and the discipline by the United States government became much more severe after 1880 as the homesteaders poured westward. The government's record was full of contradictions, stupidities, and gross indifference, not to mention frequent occasions of outright venality. A good deal of the malfeasance was just plain bumbling, but most of it originated in one way or another from the conviction that the Indian was a lower class of mankind, requiring only a minimum of human consideration.

The Indian people in their primitiveness, it is true, did not have a centralized system of government with which the whites could deal even when they wanted to. A chief was a leader only as he earned the distinction, but he was no absolute monarch in any case. He was guided by a council of headmen who achieved that status by common consent. When the white man began to tell the separate bands what they must do, the chief could only say in all honesty that he would try to persuade his men to do it. The individual warriors, and particularly the warrior societies which in some areas of activity had the real power, often did as they pleased—and often brought death and destruction to the whole tribe by their irresponsible behavior. As the white soldier chief, Bear Coat Miles, once commented, "There is no such thing as order, positive authority, or discipline among the Indian warriors."

Finally the government simply began to ignore Indian leaders who were recalcitrant, and appointed its own "chiefs," sometimes conscientious men but often mere toadies who were willing to cooperate with the white government in order to gain special favors from it.

All informed Indians knew that the supply of white soldiers was virtually inexhaustible, that they had much superior firepower, and that they had cruelly massacred Indian villages many times. Sometimes the Indians had indeed been resisting arrest, or incarceration in a reservation, or transfer to a strange environment. But on many occasions, which in the Indian mind was the rule rather than the exception, the slaughter had been utterly wanton. The Indians knew well the story of the massacre of 110 Cheyenne women and children at Sand Creek by Colonel Chivington's volunteers. They knew also of the subsequent obscene mutilation of the bodies. They knew that four years later a cavalry officer named George A. Custer, trying to recover his prestige after a year's suspension, had led an attack against Black Kettle's peaceful village on the Washita River, killing a hundred surprised warriors including the chief himself, and almost as many women and children. They knew all about Colonel Reynolds' cavalry attack on the sleeping village of Chief Two Moons, friendly toward the whites and peacefully en route to the reservation. They knew how soldiers had surrounded a village of Piegan Blackfeet on the Marias River in Montana and had slain 170 of the trapped people, including 53 women and children by the cavalry colonel's own admission.

And so on through a long list of atrocities.

Yet in spite of all this—or possibly because of it—the bulk of Great Plains Dakotas decided in the late '70s to throw themselves on the mercy of the stronger white man and accept subjugation on the prescribed reservations. They were in constant flight. They were hungry and ragged without the buffalo as their mainstay. And their women and children were always in danger of annihilation.

The Indian was losing the contest and most of them knew it. Red Cloud had been tricked into reservation life back in 1870. Sitting Bull took a flock of his Hunkpapas off to Canada and was later joined by some of Crazy Horse's Oglalas, but they were harassed by the Queen's government as well as the American, and finally in 1881 they traipsed back to the reservations—nearly 3,000 of them. Crazy Horse himself had surrendered in 1877 and was stabbed to death when he resisted being held in jail. Chief Spotted Tail and his wild Brulés were moved that same year to the Rosebud reservation, between Pine Ridge and the Missouri River, and a few years later the chief was murdered by Crow Dog, who was jealous of his power and opposed to his submissive policies.

These were all bands of the Teton Sioux. The Oglalas

numbered perhaps 7,500 and the Brulés 4,000. Along the Cheyenne River to the north, some 3,000 Tetons had been settled—mostly Minneconjous but some Blackfeet, Sans Arc, and Two Kettle. And up at Standing Rock reservation still farther north, along the Grand and Cannonball Rivers, under Sitting Bull, Gall and others, were 1,500 Hunkpapas and numerous Blackfeet Sioux and Yanktonais.

So during the Montana-Wyoming wars of 1876-77, there had been roughly 8,000 Tetons out in "hostile" territory and about an equal number settled on reservations; while by 1881, almost the entire 16,000 had come to accept incarceration on the Great Sioux Reservation, along with several thousand of their Yanktonai cousins and Cheyennes who had been displaced in the turmoil of war and forced migration.

Reservation life was debilitating both physically and morally. These were hunters and nomads, not sedentary farmers, and they could hardly be changed overnight. They were terribly susceptible to alcoholism, therefore, and there were plenty of white traders to take advantage of the weakness. They were greatly attached to their children, and resented having them hauled off by the government to distant schools which imposed strange disciplines upon them. They did not object particularly to the white man's religion; it was not so difficult to add a couple more gods to their own assortment of spirits. But for the most part they were compelled to sit around like toadstools, awaiting their meager handouts from the white agents.

Worst of all, it was humiliating enough to have to wait on the white man's patronizing charity, but when the government supplies didn't arrive because Congress had been indifferent about appropriations, or because bureaucracy bungled the shipments, or because grafters diverted it elsewhere—then the Indians simply starved. And by the end of the 1880s, these things were happening all the time. The beef issue at Pine Ridge in 1889 was down to less than half of what it had been only three years earlier. Now the wild game was gone. The only way of supplementing the food supply was through agriculture, and this dry land on which they were cooped up was little suited to growing crops of any kind. That is why it had been "given" to them, of course. Yet the agency farmers, or agricultural agents, anxious to please their superiors and hold their jobs, kept sending in fanciful reports of crop and garden production.

But even here Nature stepped in and struck an additional staggering blow. The summer of 1889 was the second year of drought on the Great Plains, and there would be still another. The grass in some areas did not adequately feed herds of cattle. The Sioux knew nothing about statistics, but as against an average annual rainfall of 36 inches in Iowa next door, or 45 inches in Washington where the Great Father lived, the Pine Ridge and Cheyenne River and Standing Rock reservations got 15 inches—and were subject to periodic devastating droughts, as even the white settlers were not long in discovering. It is semi-arid territory, much of it quite barren and part of it exactly what it is called by red men and white men alike—Bad Lands.

First the whole sweep of hunting lands from Nebraska through Wyoming to Montana had been taken away from this people; then their sacred and beloved *Paha Sapa*, the beautiful Black Hills, was rudely seized despite the signed treaties; and finally the white government proceeded to cut away other large segments of their so-called "homeland," tract by tract—9 million acres in this year of 1889 alone—leaving the little reservations shriveled and iso-lated on the dusty plains.

No wonder epidemics, mostly of the white man's diseases, began to sweep across the reservations. Already suffering from malnutrition, the children fell ready prey to measles, and even many adults died from the lack of immunity. There were periodic waves of grippe and whooping cough from which both children and adults died.

The Dakotas were a beaten and imprisoned people. They were hungry and poorly sheltered. And they were proud, anxious for some promise of deliverance from their defeat and humiliation. Since no messiah appeared amongst them, they would have to go out and find one.

In the fall of 1889, rumors began to spread of a holy man with unusual powers who had emerged somewhere far over the western mountains—the son of God returned to earth, some said, who was promising to lead all Indians everywhere out of their bondage and into a new and glorious world. The stories came to the Dakotas principal-ly by way of the Arapahos and Shoshonis of Wyoming. He was reported to be telling the Indians of a life so sweet and free that the buffalo and other game of former times would return, and all of the Indians' ancestors would be alive and happy again. The stories varied greatly, of course, as is usual in such excitement, but they kept ricocheting among the reservations from New Mexico to Montana and they would not quiet down.

At last the leaders of the Oglalas invited representatives from a few other bands to come to Pine Ridge and consider the matter with them.

Several Brulés came from the Rosebud reservation. And the Oglalas sent word to Chief Big Foot of the Minneconjous, up on the Cheyenne River, to come or send a delegate.

Big Foot sent Kicking Bear, a medicine man, born an Oglala, who had been a member of the Minneconjou band since early manhood when he married the girl, Woodpecker Woman, a niece of Big Foot's. (It was not uncommon for a young groom to join his bride's band.)

The secret council in the Indian village just outside of Pine Ridge was of such grave importance that the Oglalas took pains to share its guidance equally with both "progressive" spokesmen—those who sought actively to cooperate with the white administrators of the agency—and "nonprogressives," or those who stood aloof and noncommittal toward their white masters.

Chief Red Cloud, elder statesman of the Oglalas, and Little Wound were the principal leaders of the "nonprogressives." The "progressives" were headed by American Horse and Young-Man-Afraid-of-His-Horses. The latter two had cooperated with the Indian agents in most matters ever since coming to the reservation more than a decade earlier. Their overall posture of nonviolence and collaboration was based on the conviction that the Indian's only hope now was to persuade the white government to do what was just and honest toward its wards.

Not that these two lacked courage, however! The whites sometimes assumed that the corrupted translation, "Young-Man-Afraid-of-His-Horses," grew out of some amusing boyhood incident. But not at all. He was merely the son of

a great Oglala chief, Man-Afraid-of-His-Horse, who acquired the name not because he was afraid of anything
but, on the contrary, because he was such a renowned
terror in battle that any man who so much as saw his horse
in the distance was stricken with fright.

And American Horse also bore the name of a great chieftain who, upon surrendering before he died at Slim Buttes
in 1876, had held his gaping entrails in one hand while he
shook hands with the other—biting a stick of wood meanwhile to contain his pain. This younger American Horse
would risk his life more than once to prevent murder and
madness in the fateful year 1890.

In the end, the Oglalas appointed eight of their number
as delegates to travel westward and run down the facts
about the new Indian messiah. Good Thunder was chosen
as their leader; the others were Yellow Knife, Flat Iron,
Kicks Back, Elk Horn, Yellow Breast, Broken Arm and
Cloud Horse.

The Rosebud Brulés appointed Short Bull and Mash-the-
Kettle as their representatives.

Kicking Bear returned to Chief Big Foot on the
Cheyenne River and told him the whole story. These two
had talked together many times about the possibilities of
freeing the Indians from the white man's domination and
abuse. The chief saw the intensity of feeling in Kicking
Bear's face and voice, and he promptly appointed him his
emissary to go in search of the messiah.

Kicking Bear was a man of action, and the chief had
great confidence in him. The medicine man's traits com-
pensated for some lack of aggressiveness which Big Foot felt
in himself. The chief was a compromiser; his very rank and
prominence were based in part on a judicial habit of mind
and a capacity for peacemaking, rather than heroic
achievements in battle or holy powers and conjuring.

Big Foot was neither vainglorious nor excessively am-
bitious. Some years after his death, it was written that he
had been "wise, mild-mannered, always considerate of each
individual's rights." The recorded acts of his life confirm
this. He was physically impressive, a well-built man of
large frame. Naturally he had fought as a warrior in many
engagements during his early life—in those days he had
been called Spotted Elk—but even among the war parties
it was his sober judgment that impressed his companions,
rather than unusual fighting skills. Gradually the practice
developed of taking quarrels to Big Foot, and his reputation for the fair settlement of disputes spread to the other
bands of the western Sioux.

It is true that Chief Big Foot's father, Lone Horn, had
been a principal chief of the Minneconjous, and Big Foot
was therefore a hereditary chief. But he had begun early to
earn respect in his own right. In 1870 Chief Red Cloud
called upon him to represent the Minneconjous at a council
in Fort Laramie to determine the location of a new Teton
agency, since at this time the United States government
was still deluding the Sioux that they were to have some
voice in the matter. Dull Knife of the Northern Cheyennes
was there, and Plenty Bear of the Arapahos, and Chief
Grass representing the Blackfeet Sioux. So the young Big
Foot was among proven leaders.

At Fort Laramie he learned, along with the others, that the
government was about to shove them off into the Raw Hide
Buttes. Sitting Bull of the Hunkpapas would not even attend
the meeting, so certain was he that the government's agents
were planning some trickery. And when Red Cloud learned
what the scheme was, he ceremoniously packed up his Oglalas
and marched off to the Powder River country for the winter.

Thus the young Minneconjou leader began to size up the
white man with suspicion and mistrust.

It was in 1877, some time after his father's death, that Big Foot was persuaded to try the white man's way. The Dakotas had suffered horrible losses from the attacks of Army troops during the previous winter. Old Chief Spotted Tail of the Brulés, who with Red Cloud had now accepted confinement on a reservation, was sent to find Crazy Horse at the edge of the Big Horn Mountains and persuade him to surrender. Half of Crazy Horse's people had been frozen during the bitter winter and the remainder were now starving, but Crazy Horse walked away into the mountains and would neither see nor listen to Spotted Tail.

Big Foot and Touch-the-Clouds, however, sat and heard what Spotted Tail had to say:

"Alas! There is a time appointed to all things," the great Sioux orator and dramatist began, and he had his audience spellbound almost at once.

"Think for a moment how many multitudes of the animal tribes we ourselves have destroyed! Look upon the snow that appears today: Tomorrow it is water! Listen to the rustle of the dry leaves that were green and vigorous only a few moons before!

"We are a part of that life, and it seems that our time has come. Yet take note that the decay of one nation invigorates another. This strange white man—consider him! His gifts are many. His tireless brain, his busy hands, do wonders for his race. He is so great and so flourishing that there must be virtue and truth in his philosophy!

"I say to you, my friends, be not moved by heated arguments and revenge alone. Let us give council as old men should . . . ."

In conclusion, Spotted Tail pleaded that his hearers should come to the reservations and accept life as it is.

Big Foot was not a brilliant thinker. The oratory of
Spotted Tail and the suffering of his people persuaded
him, and he marched what was left of his Minneconjous
into Nebraska to surrender. It was only later that he
began to have bitter second thoughts.

So now in the late fall of 1889 Kicking Bear was riding
across the plains of eastern Wyoming as Chief Big Foot's
delegate, headed with his ten companions for the Wind
River agency at Fort Washakie in the heart of the Great
Mountains. Since most of the Tetons' information about
the new holy man had come to them from these neighbors, this was the obvious place to begin.

Their departure from Dakota Territory had been dis-
creetly clandestine. The officials at Pine Ridge and other
agencies frowned sharply on any wandering of this sort.
The Indians were assigned to their separate reservations,
and that was precisely where they were supposed to stay
unless they possessed written passes to travel. And these
emissaries of the Dakotas had no intention of revealing to
their white guardians the secret of a messiah who would
free them from their galling domination.

The group moved nimbly around the southern edge of
the Black Hills and was lost in the Wyoming prairies in a
couple of days. While these couriers were a thousand

miles to the west, North and South Dakota would enter the Union as states, Wyoming eight months later. But such events would have had no meaning for them, even if they had been informed, for they were dealing with vastly more heroic, earthshaking phenomena.

The delegation was moving, every mile, in quite familiar terrain. This was land for which they had fought bloody battles more than once. For roughly a decade now, about half of this Sioux nation had been trying conscientiously to adapt to the reservation life prescribed for them by the white government. The other half, although within the reservation boundaries, remained sullen, intransigent, unconvinced. Until rather recently, many eminent white men had believed in, and publicly recommended, a drastic solution of this annoyance: *Exterminate them!*

"I have come to kill Indians," Colonel John Chivington had said, "and believe it is right and honorable to use any means under God's heaven to kill Indians."

During the next few days Kicking Bear and his companions moved up the North Platte River to where it approaches the headwaters of the Powder, and after crossing the high plateau they travelled gently downhill again along the creeks leading into the Wind River.

It was stony, desolate country. As they crept toward the Indian villages around Fort Washakie, the raw wind coming down off the high mountain range tore at them fiercely, and flurries of fine snow and sleet bit their faces.

They slipped into the Indian community quietly, but before long there was feasting for the visitors and almost continuous passing of the smoking pipe. To the Tetons' surprise, other visitors had arrived just ahead of them on an identical mission. There were Northern Cheyennes from their reservation on the Tongue River in Montana, headed by a gullible medicine man named Porcupine.

They, too, wanted to know what the Arapahos and Shoshonis could tell them about the new messiah.

Chief Nakash was most expansive before his guests.

"My brothers," he cried, "let me tell you true: I went
there myself last spring. The place is far off. It is where
the Fish Eaters live, a great many days west of here.
Everything you have heard about the son of God is true.
He visits Heaven regularly and he will save us all if we
follow his teachings."

The Sioux party spent more than a week at Wind
River. At the end of their visit it was decided that Por-
cupine and two other Cheyennes, as well as several Wind
River Indians, would accompany the delegation on its
continued trip westward. The first step was to get to the
Fort Hall reservation in the Idaho country.

"We must get to the railroad," said the Shoshonis. That
meant an arduous trip straight across the Great Divide
Basin, where the water flows nowhere, to reach Rawlins
and the Union Pacific railroad. There the cars would take
them across the mountains and put them down almost at
the entrance to Fort Hall on the Snake River.

Once the decision was made, they put together a train
of ponies and pack animals and got started. Kicking Bear
and Short Bull came to understand each other intimately
during these days and nights of travel, and through their
quiet talks they developed a common philosophy about
where the Indian was headed in what was clearly going to
be a white man's world unless some drastic turnabout
could be engineered. Their discussions were frequently
filled with bitter mutterings about the loss of their old life
of freedom, about the arrogance of their white masters,
about the hunger and illness of their people, about the
shameless way in which so many onetime warriors now
accepted bribes from the white agents to spy and report

on their own people—even to don policemen's uniforms and then bully their brothers.

At last the party reached Rawlins. Kicking Bear and his companions were familiar with the railroad train, of course. Most of the supplies for the Pine Ridge agency were hauled in from the railroad at Rushville, Nebraska, by freight wagons. With a proper pass, Indians were entitled to ride on trains free in many areas of the West because of railroad easements across Indian land. But white men seldom allowed them in the coaches, so the Indians usually boarded an empty freight car or the engine tender, where discreet crewmen tended to ignore them.

Nevertheless, for most of these Dakotas and Cheyennes it was a brand new experience when they clambered aboard a westbound train at Rawlins. There was much gaping and there were some expressions of real fright in the beginning when the commotion of jerking and hissing and clanking started.

When the travelers reached Fort Hall, they found a level of excitement which none had anticipated. Several delegations of these Bannock and Shoshoni Indians had long since made the pilgrimage to the foothills of the Sierra Nevadas, to hear firsthand the message of the new Indian Redeemer. Now there was an almost continuous religious dance going on. It was called the *Dance of the Ghosts* since, the participants had been told, it would ultimately bring the spirits of all their dead forebears back to earth, alive and well again.

There was a carnival spirit everywhere, produced by the exhilaration of the new religion and the promised millenium. As far as the administrators of these western agencies were concerned, it was all relatively innocent. No overtones of rebellion had appeared in its performances. There had been a number of such religious revivals over the years, and this dance did not differ much from other Indian ceremonials except perhaps in its exhausting length.

The traveling Sioux heard a great deal about Wovoka, the Messiah, about the wonders he performed and the strictures he pronounced, but it was all strange and difficult to understand. They would see soon enough for themselves.

Their Idaho hosts were gracious and they spent six days at the village near Pocatello. Then, in the company of some newfound Bannock friends, they took another train southward to Salt Lake City. Occasionally at some junction they were forced to stop and change cars, and sometimes they would camp or be entertained at an Indian village. Everywhere they found their new friends dancing the ghost dance.

Boarding still another train at Salt Lake, Kicking Bear and his companions spent two days crossing Utah and Nevada. When they arrived at Pyramid Lake, a large crowd of Indians milled around the station—most of them strange Paiutes, but many recognizable Crows and Southern Cheyennes and men of other tribes.

The visitors were acknowledged immediately as guests. Some Fish Eaters put them in wagons and took them off to their villages at the edge of the lake, where they were made comfortable and at home. Quite naturally, their hosts spoke proudly about the Messiah.

Wovoka's story was all mixed up with the myths of various religious beliefs because he had woven it out of a patch-quilt of Indian lore and Christian instruction. At first there developed a legend that Wovoka was the son of Tavibo, a Paiute medicine man who around 1870 had stirred up the Walker Lake area. This was a mistaken assumption, but the influence of this earlier prophet on the young Wovoka was very real, as the facts demonstrate:

Tavibo, responding to the Paiutes' need for solace at the time, preached that all white men who had overrun Indian lands would one day be "swallowed up." Important to the Indian ritual of preparation for this day of judgment was a dance at night in a circle, with no fire. The dancers deliberately exhausted themselves so they could "die" and be resurrected, and therefore ready for eternal life, when all white men and turncoat Indians had been destroyed.

The Mormons were busy in this region at the same time, preaching the tenets of the Christian faith with its message of resurrection and eternal release from life's agonies. They were baptizing Bannocks and Paiutes in droves. Some observers in California and Nevada made coarse remarks about the inducement of free rations which the Mormons used, along with bland assurances that converted Indians would join the Creator's "chosen people" to establish His kingdom on earth. But in spite of this and other Christian competition, Tavibo had a considerable success until his death a few years later.

Wovoka was in his teens when Tavibo was preaching and teaching his dance, and he was deeply impressed by the whole proceedings. Many nearby tribes took up Tavibo's practices. On the Columbia River in Oregon, a prophet named Smoholla arose whose chief doctrine was that "the Red Man is going to rule this country again." Almost every Indian dreamed of this. By 1872 Smoholla's apostles were traveling to other reservations throughout the Far West, and the Indian commissioner warned:

"They have a new and peculiar religion, by the doctrines of which they are taught that a new god is coming to their rescue; that all Indians who had died heretofore, and who shall die hereafter, are to be resurrected; that as they then will be very numerous and powerful, they will be able to conquer the whites, recover their lands, and live as free and unrestrained as their fathers lived in olden times . . . . They aspire to be Indian and nothing else!"

Smoholla's followers were called "Dreamers" because of the visions of Paradise which their doctrines evoked, and the conflict between the white man and red man was considerably influenced by this movement. For example, Chief Joseph and his Nez Perces were largely under the influence of Dreamer prophets when they revolted against white control in 1877. Smoholla and a few other leaders were persuaded to go to a reservation instead of joining Chief Joseph's war, but the chief and his band were hounded all over the Northwest, their villages strewn with dead warriors and women and children after every attack, until the remnants finally surrendered.

In the following decade, still another form of hybrid evangelism showed up in the neighborhood, this time among the Indians around Puget Sound. They were known as "Shakers" because of their catatonic trembling during their dances. They used candles, bells, crucifixes and other Catholic paraphernalia in their ceremonies, copied from the missions that had come among them. The "doctors" of this religion went far south to preach among other tribes, and Wovoka had his original "revelation" at one of these sessions held by visiting evangelists.

So there was nothing new about any of this in the history of the Indians—nor, for that matter, in the history of mankind. Wovoka the Paiute happened merely to be seized with a passion to become leader of a spiritual renewal at a moment when some of his people needed and wanted a savior desperately. The turning of beaten, humiliated or enslaved peoples to such a voice is as old as the human race.

Now Kicking Bear and Short Bull were going to hear one more version of the old theme—this one pacifist in tone. But they would turn it into a doctrine of revolt and vengeance which they hoped would lead to the emancipation of the Dakotas from the white man's bondage.

In the preceding years Wovoka had been working for a white rancher, as many Paiutes did to eke out a better living than their annuities provided. The rancher was David Wilson, and Wovoka worked at his farm in spring and summer, spending the rest of the year in Indian camps or at his own lodge. From the Wilsons he learned English and some Christian worship. In the year 1887 he tried to "give the ghost dance to his people," but the Indians paid little attention at the time.

Two years later Wovoka had his great revelation. The sun "died"—that is, there happened to be a total eclipse. It occurred at a moment when Wovoka had a bad fever and was subject to delirium. He fell into a sound sleep and was taken up to "the other world." He saw God personally, he reported, as well as many people who had died long ago. They were engaged in their oldtime occupations, all happy and forever young. It was a beautiful land, full of wild game and rushing streams.

God told Wovoka to go home and tell his people to love one another. "Do not quarrel," He said, "but live peaceably with each other and with the white man. Work; do not lie or steal. Put away all of the old practices that savor of war. If men will obey these instructions faithfully, they will at last be reunited with their friends the ghosts from the other world, who will return to earth with no more death or sickness or old age."

Wovoka said that he was then "given" the dance and was commanded to bring it back to his people. The dance was to be performed at intervals throughout the next year or two, until the "renewal of the earth" took place. Dancing was to continue for five days each time—the first day for fasting and purification in the sweat baths which were characteristic of Indian religious ritual; then the dance itself was to proceed for four days.

Wovoka did not pretend at first to be "the son of God." He implied only that he was a prophet who had received a divine revelation. But as his audience and the adulation swelled, and as his fame spread until he was clearly a celebrated figure, Wovoka found it less and less convenient to straighten out the reports of his countless miracles, or to try to correct his divine relationship. And "miracles" he did perform, for he was a medicine man with some talent for conjuring tricks.

In the euphoric climate which Wovoka created around him, it is hardly surprising that endless contradictory tales emerged regarding what he did and what he said—almost as many versions as there were people listening.

Kicking Bear and his companions spent several days of delightful entertainment around Pyramid Lake, and then one morning their hosts ordered horses and wagons and announced that they were all going down to Walker Lake, nearly 100 miles to the south. "The Christ" was coming there in a few days, they said.

On the day of their arrival at Walker Lake, a great circle was cleared off not far from the Indian agency, and all the assembled throng of people gathered around—mostly Indians, but a few participating or curious whites. They waited all day, anxious to see and hear the wonder-working Messiah. Toward evening, a sudden hush went over the crowd and a group of Indians, all in white men's clothing, entered the open area from one side, surrounding the Great One as he walked along. When they reached the center of the circle, Wovoka sat down and bowed his head while a great fire was built close by him.

Porcupine the Cheyenne was stricken almost dumb, but not quite. "I thought the Great Father was a white man," he said to Short Bull in a loud whisper, "but this man looks like an Indian!"

Finally the Messiah arose and the audience sat silent. It was almost dark, but the bonfire reflected light on his face. Looking around the circle, he began to speak slowly:

"My children, I am very glad to see you all. I sent for you and you have come. I am going to talk to you after a while about your relatives who are dead and gone."

He stood for a little while, his hands folded carelessly together. "My children, I want you to listen to everything I have to say. I will teach you, also, how to dance a dance, and I want you to dance it faithfully from now on.

"In another spring or two the Great Spirit is coming. He is going to bring back game of every kind, so that it will be thick everywhere. All dead Indians will come to life and live among us again. They will all be strong and young again. Old, blind Indians will be able to see again.

"When the Great Spirit comes this way, all Indians will go away up high into a land where no one can hurt them any more. A big flood will come and all the evil people will be drowned. They will die. Later the water will go away and there will be no one but good people anywhere. All kinds of game will be plentiful.

"Now I want you to get the word to all Indians every-where to keep dancing until this time of judgment comes."

After a while the Indian Christ began a dance, the one that was being called the "ghost dance." Instead of mere rhythmic steps sideways, which the Indians were ac-customed to, the Messiah showed them how to take quick steps forward and back, then sideways. It was more vigorous, more demanding, than most of the common In-dian dances. And the dancers were required to hold hands tightly all the time so as to keep an unbroken circle.

Wovoka himself led the dance for a while, then he lay down, but many of the Indians danced for hours. Finally they began to fall, exhausted. And later when they awoke, many were able to report incredible visions and experi-ences. Good Thunder told his companions that Chasing Hawk, an Oglala who had died not long before, had in-vited him into his tepee, and that one of his own dead sons had spoken to him there.

After his talk to the people on the second evening, Wovoka walked among the visitors, handing them paints for their faces and sagebrush twigs to spread in their sweat lodges. He came directly up to Good Thunder and said, "Use these before each dance; they will give you pleasure."

Good Thunder, face to face with deity, was speechless.

"My children," said the Messiah, turning to the crowd, "when you get home, go to farming and send your children to school. Do nothing wrong, and especially do not steal. People cannot take anything away with them when they die. And whisky is bad; those who drink it cause murders and suicides. Someday our Father, God, will look down and those who have done wrong will be shaken from the earth.

"Now my Father had a purpose in sending me to the Indians. I came to visit the white people first, but they killed me, and you can see the marks of my wounds on my feet, hands, and on my back."

Actually Wovoka was wearing moccasins and a white duster, but of course the visitors stared at his hands, and there, sure enough, were distinct wounds.

"My Father has given you back your old life," he went on. "When you get home I want you to tell your people to follow my example. Any Indian who does not obey me will be buried under a new land which will grow over this old one when the earth is renewed. You people, all of you, use the paints and sagebrush I have given you. In the spring when the grass is green, your people who have gone before will all return, and you will see all your old friends because you came at my bidding. Even the buffalo, if you should kill one, will come to life again if you leave the head, the tail, and the feet."

Months later when the travelers had returned home and told this story innumerable times, they began to recall that they had indeed slaughtered a buffalo and eaten what they wanted, whereupon the buffalo arose and went on its way. Also during the journey homeward they had called on the Messiah for help because they were so weary and home-sick, and the next morning they discovered that they were much farther along than when they had fallen asleep!

Short Bull and Kicking Bear, being medicine men themselves, kept their own counsel during the days at Walker Lake, but the potential of the ghost dance did not escape either of them. When Wovoka spoke of "evil people" who were going to be destroyed, he was surely refering to the white people who had upset the Indians' lives so calamitously! And since all Indians were going to be reborn after another spring or two, risking one's life became far more inviting.

The Dakotas spent many days listening to Wovoka's

sermons and dancing the ghost dance. Toward the end of their stay, the Messiah said one day, "I am not lying to you, my children; I made everything on this earth. I was taken up to Heaven to see your dead friends, and I saw my own father and mother there. In the beginning, after God made the earth, they sent me down to teach people. But the people were afraid of me and treated me badly. I did not try to defend myself. I found my children were bad, so I left them and went back to Heaven. I told them that after so many years I would come back to see my children, so now at the end of that time I have been sent back here to try to teach them. My father told me that the earth was getting old and worn out, and that I was to renew everything as it used to be and make it better."

This "renewal of the earth" about which Wovoka spoke regularly produced different images in the minds of his hearers. Kicking Bear saw a giant so tall that his head was in the clouds, spreading rich black loam "to a depth five times the height of a man" across the whole landscape to replace the dry, baked clay of the arid prairies. His daydream pictured all Indians being lifted up and suspended while the "wave of new earth" passed under them, after which they were set down in lush fields of grass and in forests abundant with wildlife.

Good Thunder had a similar vision. All of the white people, he said, were to be buried under the wave of new, good earth, so that they could no longer bother the Indians, who would all be saved. Another of the pilgrims, remembering Wovoka's earlier words, thought that all Indians were to be taken up into the high mountains while a flood drowned all white men. And still another described the coming cosmic cataclysm as a tornado in which all whites would be swept away to oblivion, while Indians stood untouched.

Imaginings of this sort flowed through the minds of Wovoka's visitors constantly as they listened to his ambiguities day after day, then their attention would be caught again and he would be saying:

"When you fight, that is bad. We must all be friends with each other. The white man and the Indian are brothers. If you are all good, I will send people among you who will heal all of your wounds and sickness by merely touching you, and then you will live forever. Do not quarrel, or strike each other, or shoot each other.

"Now if any man disobeys me, his tribe will be wiped off the face of the earth. Believe in everything I say. Do not doubt me or say that I have lied, for if you do I will know it. I will know your thoughts and actions no matter what part of the world you may be in."

So the indoctrination and the visions and the dancing went on for several weeks, and finally it came time for the Dakotas and their companions to start home. Porcupine was so exhilarated by the whole experience that when he got back to his village near the Tongue River agency in Montana, he was persuaded that he himself had a touch of divinity, and word got around the plains that the Cheyennes had their own messiah. But his enthusiasm was deflated some when he found an overwhelming majority of nonbelievers among his own people—a characteristic experience for messiahs.

Said Porcupine, "When I heard this from the Christ and came back to tell it to my people, I thought they would listen. . . . I knew my people were bad and had heard nothing of this, so I got them together and told them of it and warned them to listen for their own good. I talked to them for four days and four nights. . . ."

Kicking Bear, Short Bull and their companions returned to Pine Ridge in March of 1890. The new messianic promise arrived among these Sioux Indians just when they were beginning to feel most depressed by the latest contraction of their reservations and by their shrunken food allowances. More and more they were dreaming of the joys they had known in the freedom of their old life.

But immediately the delegation to Wovoka began to run into difficulties. Tipped off to the excitement getting started at Pine Ridge, Agent Hugh Gallagher promptly called in Good Thunder to ask where he had been these last few months and what this story he was telling his people was all about.

Good Thunder persisted in his silence.

"Look, my friend," said the agent, "I'm going to find out what's going on here if it takes a month, so you had better start talking before I have to put you in jail."

But Good Thunder would not utter a word of confirmation or explanation. In frustration, Gallagher sent him and two other apparent leaders in the excitement to the agency jail. They were held for two days. Then, although they were still adamant, they were freed with a stern warning.

Good Thunder did not like the inside of a jail at all. The Teton Sioux could not tolerate incarceration. So Good Thunder decided to postpone for the moment any further councils on the coming of the Messiah.

On the Rosebud reservation, Short Bull and Mash-the-Kettle also began to hold meetings to tell the story. Very little was said about Wovoka's pacifist admonitions, but a great deal was made of the early destruction of all white men, who had treated the Messiah so abominably on his earlier visit. And great emphasis was put on the necessity for continuous ghost-dancing so as to identify the faithful and be ready for the millenium.

Agent George Wright was not long in hearing about all this, and he sent his Indian police to sit at the meetings and report to him. When he heard the tone of the message, he ordered Short Bull into his office.

"My son, I will tell you right at the start that you or anybody else who promises this kind of nonsense and stirs up your people with it is going to be put in prison. Already you have got the Brulés so disturbed that they are not paying attention to their livestock or preparing for spring farm work. You are going to be at fault if the planting is not done on time and your relatives go hungry next fall. You must know that the Great Father and all his people are not going to be wiped out; there are thousands upon thousands of them in the East. Now I want a promise from you that this will stop."

Short Bull hung his head and looked at the floor. He was unsure of himself as a combatant in such matters. Although a medicine man, he was dealing here with gigantic new forces and he must proceed cautiously.

"All right," he said, "I will stop for now."

He needed time to think, and also he needed to talk to Kicking Bear and the others. If the ghost dance was to be staged, it plainly would have to be done in secrecy, well away from the agent's spying police.

But Kicking Bear was not going to be much help at present. Upon his return to the Cheyenne River, he reported at great length to Chief Big Foot and his council of headmen. Here again, the emphasis was all on arousing the people to defy their white masters, the ghost dance providing the most pleasurable and effective symbol of this posture. The risks were small, he pointed out. Had not the Messiah promised that succor was at hand?

Big Foot did not quite understand how this distant Messiah was going to bring it all about, but he reveled in the promise nevertheless. He was furious with the white government because the territory connecting him with his Oglala brothers had been taken away from the Indians by the previous year's land commission, and he was equally outraged at the continuing diminution of rations when his people were already short of supplies and hungry, many of them ill.

Emboldened by Kicking Bear's fiery message of hope and defiance, Chief Big Foot called his band together and invited them to go up the Cheyenne River to Deep Creek—as far away from the agency on the Missouri River as they could get without risking interference from the soldiers in the Black Hills. There, he announced, they would establish a new village.

But this got action faster than Big Foot had anticipated. Agent Charles McChesney was not sure what his wards were up to, and he dared not let them interfere with white settlement of the new land opened up for homesteading. So he called for soldiers, and late in April Captain A. G. Henissee was sent out from Fort Meade, close to the Black Hills, with three troops of cavalry and two of infantry, to set up a "camp of observation" at the Cheyenne Forks, just eight miles above the new Minneconjou village. As long as Chief Big Foot stayed on the Cheyenne, the government decided not to bother him at present.

Kicking Bear now sent messages to several other agencies, inviting the leaders to come to the Cheyenne River for a grand council at which the ghost dance would be taught.

But already Good Thunder and Short Bull had been humbled, and there was no response.

Kicking Bear sensed the dangers around him and decided to go back to Wind River in Wyoming and see how the ghost dance was progressing there. So at Cheyenne River, also, things quieted down. And although Big Foot was disappointed, he had no choice but to await further developments. Meanwhile, the story of the Messiah was traveling around the reservations. A third summer of drought—the worst yet—was about to arrive.

A fullblown explosion of the ghost dance was not far ahead.

CHAPTER II

THE MESSAGE

Kicking Bear returned in mid-July from his self-imposed exile among the Arapaho ghost dancers. He had always been an accomplished orator, although not a very good organizer, and he was now ready to deliver "The Message." The fanaticism of the Arapaho ghost dancers had persuaded him that there was no longer any need to be timid.

He came to the Pine Ridge reservation and stood on a hill alongside White Clay Creek, looking down at the metropolis which the agency had become. In the center bracketing the road or main street was the village proper—a hotel, several trading posts, the official agency buildings, two churches, the day school and a larger boarding school, employees' apartments, and so on. Around the fringe was a rough circle of cabins—mostly mixed-blood traders, scouts, and freight-haulers. Along the creek west of town and running south for several miles were the Indian camps—old Chief Red Cloud's village nearest, marked by a two-story house which the government had built for him, Red Shirt's camp just beyond, and then numerous others.

Kicking Bear decided that the agency itself, under such close control by the agent and his police, was not the most fertile ground for what he had to do, and he turned down the creek toward the northwest for a dozen miles until he reached No Water's village. There he was received enthusiastically. No Water was especially angry about the limited number of beef cattle that were being allotted each month to his people from the government herd. He told everyone who would listen that "they are deliberately starving us to death. . . . It is a plan!"

Kicking Bear's highly embellished description of the ghost dance among the Arapahos, and its promise of more dramatic things to come, set No Water's camp ablaze in short order. Within a day or two, a ghost dance was going full tilt.

By the first of August, Kicking Bear had transferred his tutoring to other parts of the Pine Ridge agency. Knife Chief, Iron Bird and Whetstone had a joint camp on Porcupine Creek now, with about 150 dancers active most of the time. Under Kicking Bear's supervision, Torn Belly and Jack Red Cloud, the chief's son, took their followers out along White Clay Creek and set up another dance with some 600 performers.

Kicking Bear was beginning to feel his importance. So spontaneous was his success as a prophet and evangelist proving to be among the Oglalas, he was determined to exploit it to the hilt while the climate was favorable. After all, the Oglalas were going to be the critical element in any effective resistance. Big Foot's band of Minneconjous was small by comparison. Furthermore, the pressure had to be focussed against the Pine Ridge agency, which was the obvious center of white power. The United States government sometimes ignored, for considerable periods of time, what was going on in the hinterland along the Cheyenne River and elsewhere, but it never relaxed for a moment its hold at Pine Ridge.

The apostle finally went to Little Wound's village on Medicine Root Creek, 40 miles northeast of Pine Ridge. By this time he had his message perfected, his oratory was getting results, and he did not change its tone thereafter.

"My brothers," he would call out, "I bring you the promise of a day when there will be no white man to lay his hand on the bridle of any Indian's horse—"

This rallying cry against the master race was exactly the right way to begin, and his audience shouted "Hau! Hau!" in approval.

"I bring you the promise of a day when the Red Men of the prairie will rule the world, and will not be turned from their hunting-grounds by any man—"

"Hau! Hau! Hau!" came the response again.

"I bring you a message from your fathers, the ghosts. They asked me to tell you that they are now marching to join you, led by the Messiah who came once to live on earth with the white men—but they cast him out and killed him!

"I have seen the wonders of the Spirit Land, and have talked with the ghosts. I traveled far. Now I am sent back with this message: Get ready for the coming of the Messiah and the return of the ghosts next spring!"

Kicking Bear's audience howled its excitement, and he timed his pause carefully before continuing.

"In my tepee on the Cheyenne reservation, I arose many moons ago and prepared for a long journey. I had been told by a voice to go forth and meet the ghosts, because they were preparing to return and inhabit the earth. I traveled on the iron cars of the white man until I came to the place where the railroad ends. There I met two Indians whom I had never seen before, but who greeted me as a brother and gave me meat and bread. They had horses, and we rode without talking for four days, for I knew they would be witnesses to what I would see.

"Two suns we had traveled and had passed the last sign of white men—for no white man had the courage to travel so far!—when we saw a strange and fierce-looking black man, dressed in skins. He lived alone, and had medicine with which he could do anything he wished. He would wave his hands and make great heaps of money.

Or he would make another motion, and there before us would be many spring wagons, all painted and ready to hitch horses to. And still another motion of his hands and there sprung up before us great herds of buffalo!"

Most of Kicking Bear's listeners by now had their mouths open in wonderment, and he hurried along.

"The black man spoke to us and told us that he was a friend of the Indian, that we should remain with him and go no farther, and that we could have all we wanted of the money, spring wagons, and buffalo.

"But we saw that we were being tempted from our purpose, and so our hearts were turned away from the black man, my brothers. We left him, and traveled for two more days.

"On the evening of the fourth day, when we were weak and faint from our journey, we looked for a camping place and were met by a man who was dressed like an Indian, but whose hair was long and glistening like the yellow money of the white man. His face was beautiful, and when he spoke my heart was glad and I forgot my hunger and the toil I had gone through. He said, 'Hau, my children, you have done well to make this long journey to come here. Leave your horses and follow me.'

"And our hearts sang in our breasts. And he led us up a great ladder of small clouds until we followed him through an opening in the sky—"

Kicking Bear was silent for a few seconds, but there was not a sound anywhere.

"My brothers, the tongue of Kicking Bear is straight, but he cannot tell all that he saw, because he is not an orator, but only the forerunner and herald of the ghosts. The one whom we followed took us to the Great Spirit and his wife, and we lay prostrate on the ground, but I saw that they were dressed as Indians!

"Then from an opening in the sky we were shown all the countries of the earth, and the camping-grounds of our fathers since the beginning. All were there—the tepees, the ghosts of our fathers, the great herds of buffalo, and a country that smiled because it was lush and rich. . . . And the white man was not there!"

A few of the enraptured listeners found their voices to murmur "Hau, hau!" in subdued tones.

"Then he who led us showed us his hands and feet, and there were wounds in them which had been made by the white men when he went to them and they crucified him. And he told us he was going to come on earth again, only this time he would remain and live with the Indians, because they were his chosen people!

"Then we were seated on rich skins, from animals which were unknown to me, in front of the open door of the Great Spirit's tepee. And we were told how to say the prayers and perform the dance that I have now come to show my brothers. And the Great Spirit spoke to us, saying:

" 'Take this message to my red children and tell it to them as I say it. I have neglected the Indians for many moons, but now I will make them my people if they obey me in this message. The earth is getting old and I will make it new for my chosen people, the Indians, who are going to inhabit it. And among them will be all of their ancestors who have died, their fathers, mothers, brothers, cousins and wives—all those who hear my voice through the tongues of my children.

" 'I will cover the earth with new soil to the depth of five times the height of a man, and under this new soil will be buried all of the whites. And all the holes with rotten places will be filled up. The new lands will be covered with sweet-grass and running water and trees. Herds of buffalo and ponies will stray over it, that my red children may eat and drink, hunt, and rejoice. And the sea to the west I will fill up, so that no ships may pass over it, and the other seas I will make impassable also.

" 'And while my children are dancing and preparing to join the ghosts, they shall have no fear of the white man, for I will take from him the secret of making gunpowder! And any gunpowder they have on hand will not burn when it is directed against my children, the red people, who have learned the song and dance of the ghosts. But the powder which my children have will burn and kill when it is directed against the white man by those who believe! And if a red man should die at the hands of a white while he is dancing, his spirit will only go to the end of the earth, join the ghosts of his fathers, and then return to his friends the next spring!'

"So the Great Spirit said to us, 'Go, then, my children, and tell these things to all the people, and get ready for the coming of the ghosts next spring.' "

Now Kicking Bear paused to let these marvels sink in, and then he lowered his voice dramatically and concluded:

"We were given food that was rich and sweet to taste. As we sat there eating, up through the clouds came a man as tall as a tree and as thin as a snake, with great teeth sticking out of his mouth and his body covered with short hair, and we knew at once that this was the Evil Spirit. And he said to the Great Spirit, 'I want half of the people of the earth!' And the Great Spirit replied, 'No, I cannot give you any. I love them all too much.' The Evil Spirit asked again, and again he was refused. He asked a third time, and the Great Spirit then told him he could have the whites, to do with them as he wished, but he could not have any Indians because they were the chosen people for all future time.

"Then we were shown the dance and we were taught the songs that I am now bringing to you, my brothers, and we were led down the ladder of clouds by the same one who led us up. We found our horses and rode back to the railroad, the Messiah flying along through the air with us and teaching us the songs for the new dances. At the railroad he left us and told us to return to our people and tell all the red nations what we had seen. And he promised us that he would return to the clouds no more, but would remain at the end of the earth and lead the ghosts of our fathers to meet us as soon as this next winter has passed."

The weight of this stupendous pronouncement was almost more than Little Wound's people could bear, and the community fell into an uproar of discussion and conjecture.

Little Wound, who at this time was 62 years of age, went into his cabin by himself and reflected a long time on what Kicking Bear had told. Just before sunset he came out and called the people together. When they were quiet he said, "My friends, if this is a good thing we should have it. If it is not, it will fall to the ground by itself. So you had better learn this dance of Kicking Bear's, and then if the Messiah does come, he will not pass us by but help us to get back our hunting-grounds and buffalo."

Already Little Wound was three-fourths persuaded by Kicking Bear's oratory. Before long, 300 of his people were staging regular ghost dances, and he himself was relating at great length his visits with the Great Spirit during his trances. He even outdid Kicking Bear's fanciful drama in one respect:

"Wakan-tanka told me personally that the earth was now bad and worn out. He said we needed a new dwelling place where the rascally whites could not disturb us. So he instructed me to return to my people, the Lakotas, and tell them that if they would be constant in the dance, and pay no attention to the whites, he would shortly come to our aid. If the high priests would make medicine-shirts for the dancers and pray over them, no harm could come to the wearer. The bullets of any whites who tried to stop the ghost dance would fall to the ground without doing anyone harm, and the person who fired such shots would drop dead!"

The seed for this part of the hallucination had been planted by Kicking Bear himself. Speaking privately with Little Wound, he had told of the white shirts which Wovoka and his aides wore to ward off evil influences or other harm to the faithful ghost dancers. Wovoka plainly had got the idea from the clerical uniforms worn by Catholic and Mormon missionaries, and adapted by the Shakers and others.

To Little Wound it seemed natural that if holy-shirts would ward off evil, they would certainly stop the white man's bullets, which were the worst evil of all. The idea served Kicking Bear's purposes splendidly, and he picked up the theme at once. Ghost-shirts for the warriors and ghost-dresses for the women shortly became commonplace among the ghost dancers. They were usually made of white muslin which could be painted, front and back, with the necessary colors—blue across the back with a straight yellow line alongside, and always the picture or symbol of an eagle.

"The Great Spirit said he had prepared a hole in the ground filled with hot water and fire," continued Little Wound, "to receive all white men and nonbelievers. . . ."

Little Wound's people were terrified by the prospect of such a fate if they failed to conform. They danced madly until many foamed at the mouth, dropping in exhaustion to "die" and meet their lost loved ones, or staggering around like drunken persons. As the days and nights were still hot, the dancers usually fell within a half hour or so after the violent performances began. Stimulated by the zeal to be more than ready when the Messiah came, they clawed at the air with wild contortions and threw themselves about while howling dismal chants. The ground was soon strewn with immobile bodies.

Kicking Bear introduced the practice of calling a council of participants, after they had returned to consciousness, at which they would testify in turn as to their visions or experiences in the other world. Very few admitted that they hadn't seen a thing.

From Medicine Root Creek, Kicking Bear went down to the camp of Big Road and Good Thunder on Wounded Knee Creek. Good Thunder had been apprehensive about starting up the dance after his jailing by Agent Gallagher, but Kicking Bear's presence stiffened his backbone and they soon had some 250 men and women dancing there.

The warriors usually went through purification rites for several hours preceding these dances. The sweat bath was an old Indian institution connected with the Sun Dance and other rites, and the ghost dance sites were often littered with skin-covered sweat lodges where the Indian women or medicine men would pour water on the heated stones to produce the necessary steam. Then, purified, the warrior would paint his face for the dance as Wovoka had ordered.

Needless to say, Agent Gallagher was hearing about all of this frenzied activity, and he was disturbed. Late in August he sent some of his Indian police to Torn Belly's camp on the White River with orders to stop the dance and send the people home. The police came back and said that the dancers would pay no attention to them. So the next day Gallagher went himself, accompanied by twenty Indian police and Interpreter Philip Wells.

There was an American flag flying from the prayer pole in the center of the dance ring, but not a soul was in sight. The inhabitants and the visiting dancers had all run and hid in a nearby grove. After a minute, two Indians emerged from the brush and each dropped on one knee, pointing their Winchesters directly at the police.

Gallagher was incensed.

"Arrest those two Indians," he commanded sharply.

Wells translated the order to the police and then continued in Siouan, "That is his order, but I suggest you all stand perfectly still."

Agent Gallagher started forward on his mount, assuming his police would move with him. Instead, Wells, who himself was part Indian, circled his horse in front of the Indian agent to shield him and slow him down. Other Indians' heads began to appear above the creek bank, the muzzles of their guns erect at their sides.

"What do you mean by drawing guns on me when I come here as your agent?" Gallagher cried to the Indian nearest him.

Wells translated the question and then added, "Look here, father, I want you to obey me. Put that gun down and come here."

The two men knew each other, and the Indian laid his gun on the ground.

"Yes, my son," he said quietly, "I will obey you." Then he turned to the Indian agent. "If you have come to talk to me as a father, why have you brought so many men with guns?"

When Wells translated, Gallagher stammered out, "Don't take offense! The police are required to carry their weapons wherever they go."

Meanwhile, more Indians had arisen along the creek bank and some were levelling their rifles. One of them called out a taunt to the Indian police, who had begun nervously to draw their pistols from their belts.

Not a second too soon, Young-Man-Afraid-of-His-Horses, one of Gallagher's policemen, rode forward and called out, "Brothers, we are only here to talk. Don't do anything foolish!"

Torn Belly's men respected him, and slowly their guns were lowered. Wells hastily explained to the warriors near him that the agent had no intention of interfering with the ceremony—that he had come merely to see what the ghost dance was all about. If Gallagher understood any of this, he decided that it would not be discreet to dispute it.

Soon Torn Belly himself walked up out of the woods. Interested now only in saving the agent's life and his reputation, Wells told Torn Belly that Gallagher would like to have a council at the agency the following week to discuss the ghost dance.

The chief was suspicious, and grinned as if to say, "We both know what kind of a dressing-down I would get there, don't we?" But in Siouan he said, "I do not like the idea, but I will leave it to my headmen."

So he and some of the men turned back into the woods and held a short meeting, after which he came forward and said, "They agree!" Then he shook hands all around and called out, "But now stay and watch our dance!" And before Gallagher could respond, the Indians were pouring into the dance circle. Within minutes the chain of dancers was threshing in a most violent manner. Gallagher was even more startled by the ferocity of it than he had anticipated. Mere police orders and slaps on the wrist were not going to stop this thing, he thought to himself.

But he had learned only a day or two earlier that he was about to be relieved of his post as agent and replaced by a political appointee. A new administration in Washington was madly collecting its spoils. He could not see that any purpose would be served by getting his head blown off in his last few weeks here.

It was about this same time that Short Bull, quiet in the Rosebud all summer, began to recover his courage and get the new religion organized in the Brulé country. By mid-September the ghost dance was going on in a half-dozen camps around the reservation. Schoolteachers reported that the children were not coming to school because they were attending ghost dances and preparing for the promised millenium. The district farmers, or agricultural agents, complained that the livestock was unattended and truck gardens were full of weeds, although in the dusty soil there was mighty little to harvest and store anyway. One family near Hidden Timber had nursed a single row of potatoes running along the bottom of a dry gulch for an eighth of a mile, but the potatoes, when finally dug up, were about the size of cherries.

When the Brulés came into the agency to get their bimonthly rations, a rumor spread around that soldiers were coming. The ghost dancers raced to their homes, stripped to their breechcloths, slapped on war paint, and rode en masse down the road a dozen miles toward the railroad to await battle. Agent Wright followed them and persuaded the warriors, after several hours of argument, that the rumor was false. But the incident revealed the explosive temper of his wards, and he decided stern measures were called for.

He returned to the agency and called together all the Indians who were still there.

"My sons, I want to tell you that this nonsense is going to stop, right now. I am not going to issue any more rations to anyone until it does. Now you can go home and tell your villages to take their choice. Either stop the dancing or don't bother to come again for rations, because I will not issue any!"

Within two weeks, the great majority of ghost dancers were out of food and ready to capitulate. But at this stage the government bureaucracy took charge. A census-taker said he could find only 5,250 Indians on the Rosebud reservation, while Wright had been drawing the diminished rations for 7,500. The Indian bureau's inspector concluded that Wright had been pocketing the difference, and had him removed.

The special agent sent in to take Wright's place knew nothing about handling the Brulés, and they went berserk in their ghost-dancing. Much of the agency's breeding stock was slaughtered for food, and many of the Indians spent every dollar they could accumulate for guns and ammunition.

Wright was exonerated and returned to his post less than three months later, but by that time the explosion had already occurred.

Despite Chief Big Foot's reputation for moderation and wisdom, his mild manner scarcely concealed his frequent irritation over the arrogance of the white government toward his people. He felt a deep sense of responsibility for his Minneconjous. Like Kicking Bear, he racked his mind with the problem of what was happening to the Indians as a race, and what alternatives there were to governance by white masters. He loved the traditional life he had known as a young man, and he was disinclined to give it up without the most determined struggle. And yet the implications of this course conflicted distressingly with his wish always for pacifist solutions.

The same dilemma confronted the whole western Sioux nation, of course. The collaborationist half sought only to avoid trouble with the white man. They bowed meekly to every whim of the Indian agent, and stayed close to the agency both for protection and to win special favors. This infuriated the more belligerent warriors, who felt it essential to resist white power at every turn. The schism between these two policies was so deep, so fundamental, that quarrels developed constantly within villages and even within families.

Since midsummer when the ghost dance began separating bands into these conflicting camps, the leaders at Pine Ridge had realized that this division must lead ultimately to the further weakening and disintegration of the Indians' position. Someone suggested that Big Foot be brought in to see whether he couldn't help reunify the Teton bands on a common, middle-ground course. It did not occur to them that Big Foot himself was deep in emotional turmoil over this same problem. And because he could arrive at no satisfactory solution, he found himself driven more and more to temporizing—to seeking escape from the dilemma rather than bold confrontation with it.

Big Foot was resigned to the probability that he would never be one of the great, long-remembered Sioux chieftains—he was not a Gall, or a Spotted Tail, a Crazy Horse, a Red Cloud. Actually, although a good many hundred Minneconjous considered him their chief, his own village was a small one—only one-third the size of Hump's, who lived next door to him at Cherry Creek.

Both Red Cloud and Hump managed somehow to stay close to the white men without abandonment of their pride as Indians. Many of the Oglalas, it is true, did not think much of old Red Cloud any more; he was too submissive to the whites in his fine house at Pine Ridge and his fancy team and buggy which the agent maintained for him. But he continued to display a sullen attitude toward the whites before his own people, and thus avoided the taint of abject surrender.

And Hump, for years, had shown up alternately on one side of the fence and then the other. When he surrendered a year or two after the Little Big Horn battle, he became a scout for Colonel Nelson A. Miles and served the bluecoats so well that he was later made chief of police on the Cheyenne River reservation. Then in 1889, wearing his police uniform, he led some of the fiercest opposition to the Crook commission's proposal to take more land away from the Dakotas and break up the Great Sioux reservation. But when he discovered that the Indians were going to lose anyway, he himself turned around and signed the repugnant treaty.

Another of these chameleon-like performances was now about to anger and permanently alienate his old friend, Big Foot.

A profound question haunted Big Foot with which he was unable to cope. What wrong had the Indian done that the Great Spirit had sent these hordes of whites, with their powerful weapons, to drive the Red Man from his traditional lands, causing him to starve unless he accepted the white man's crumbs? Was this truly a sign from our natural mother, Earth, that the Indian was of no consequence in the scheme of things?

No, no! How could any self-respecting Dakota warrior accept such a degrading conclusion? On the contrary, was not this anguish a test of the Indian's mettle, perhaps, intended to call forth supreme exhibitions of perseverance and skillful use of the helpful medicine which the Great Spirit would provide if the Red Man was alert and ready to exploit it? That Wakan-tanka would do less for his people was unthinkable!

Into this agitation in Big Foot's heart came Kicking Bear at last, with the ghost dance and its hopeful promise. When the prophet had finished his evangelizing on the Pine Ridge reservation and began organizing the dance along the Cheyenne River, Big Foot's village on Deep Creek almost doubled in size in about two weeks. Minneconjou widows and their families from settlements through-

out the reservation swarmed to the Big Foot camp upon
hearing that a great medicine man in the West was promising to bring back their deceased husbands and fathers.

Kicking Bear divided his time for a while between the
Big Foot village and Hump's, 25 miles down the Cheyenne. The ghost dance became a rage at both places.

Hump, like Little Wound, went the whole way. He
peeled off his police uniform and donned a ghost-shirt, in-
timating that he was ready personally to prove his in-
vulnerability to the white man's bullets. Visitors from
other agencies now began drifting in to hear the Messiah's
words directly from Apostle Kicking Bear's mouth, and
they fed the dance. Agent Perain Palmer, a newly appointed administrator replacing McChesney, sent out his
Indian police several times with orders to put a stop to
these goings-on, but without result.

At Standing Rock reservation another hundred miles to
the north, Sitting Bull was fuming. Several times he had
asked Agent James McLaughlin, a tough old professional
in the Indian service, for permission to go down to
Cheyenne River for a visit. The agent knew all too well
what the attraction was, and he not only refused permission but began installing his police at strategic points to
watch Sitting Bull's every movement. He made it plain to

the Indian commissioner that Standing Rock would never be a quiet place again until Sitting Bull and his more radical associates were sent elsewhere.

After the ghost dance had set the Cheyenne River hills afire, Sitting Bull sent a delegation to ask Kicking Bear to come to Grand River. And early in October, reveling now in his fame, Kicking Bear went.

His presence there was immediately reported to Agent McLaughlin, who sent out a squad of fourteen Indian police to ride Kicking Bear off his reservation. Headed by Crazy Walking, the policemen got there in the middle of the prophet's story of the Messiah, and they were so awed by it that they almost forgot why they were there. When they remembered, the best they could do was to ask Sitting Bull ever so politely to send his guest back home.

"Maybe tomorrow," said Sitting Bull.

Incensed by this response, McLaughlin the next day sent one of his trusted lieutenants, an Indian named Chatka, to Grand River. There was a large ghost dance in progress when Chatka arrived, and the Indians were in a frenzy, but the lieutenant walked straight to the center of the dance circle.

"Kicking Bear, my brother," he called out, "how many of your people are here from Cheyenne River?"

"I have six companions," said Kicking Bear soberly. "How many police do you have?"

Chatka had exactly one man with him. He had insisted that he didn't want to be bothered with more.

"Never mind that," he replied. "I can get all that are necessary. I want you and your friends from Cheyenne River to come with me now and mount your ponies."

The evangelist sensed that Chatka meant business. With Sitting Bull looking on and not in a mood to interfere, Kicking Bear and his men followed the policemen out of the

circle and went to where their horses were tethered. Chatka
and his aide rode with them all the way to the Moreau
River, where they were within the Cheyenne River reservation again. Then, raising his hand in farewell, Chatka
watched the Minneconjous ford the river and disappear.

As soon as the party had left his village, Sitting Bull
thought what a fool he had been made, and tried to con-
ceive something to counteract the humiliation quickly.
He went to his cabin and dug out the peace pipe which
he had smoked with the white commander at Fort
Buford when he returned from Canada to surrender,
nine years earlier. Returning to the circle, he stood on a
box and called out for the ghost dancers to listen.

"Do you see what I have here? It is my most sacred
possession. With it I pledged a life of peace to the white
man. But the pledge is no longer any good because of the
way the white man has betrayed us and humiliated us,
and I will show you what I think of my life in the struggle now approaching. . . ."

He held the pipe high in both hands and broke it.
The ghost dancers howled and returned to their per-
formance. Sitting Bull kept them at it almost continuously thereafter, as long as there were fanatics capable
of dancing. At every opportunity he publicly insulted
the Indian policemen who lived nearby, and he
frequently would sit for hours, sullen and un-
communicative.

At the end of October, both Sitting Bull and Big Foot
got word of two impressive examples of defiance toward
their white overseers. The Indian leaders were increas-
ingly on tenterhooks, and every insult to the whites was
assuming great importance to them.

The first of these challenges took place at Pine Ridge.
The agent appointed to succeed Gallagher there, a local

politician named Daniel Royer, knew that the situation was unmanageable—at least by him—and he was pleading continuously with Washington for armed forces to take over control. But short of actual desperation, the civilian Bureau of Indian Affairs was little interested in acknowledging its impotency and throwing its wards into the waiting arms of the military.

General Miles, commanding the Division of the Missouri, happened to be making a routine visit to Pine Ridge at this time to investigate another matter. He asked for a council of Indian leaders and started to give them a fatherly lecture about good behavior. Little Wound, at whose village on Medicine Root Creek the ghost dance had been going on steadily for two months, arose and asked for the floor.

"My father, the great Chief Bear Coat," he said through the interpreter, "I am getting tired of hearing how all of us Indians ought to quit being Indians and start being white people; how we ought to do everything we are told, just because the white man tells us to. We are Indians, and we are not going to stop being Indians no matter what is done to us. Nor should we stop. We have a right to be what we are. We should behave like Indians and live like Indians."

He waited for the translation to be completed. A somewhat sober, puzzled look came over General Miles' previously smiling face. Then Little Wound continued:

"We can remain Indians by dancing the new ghost dance, and all of you chiefs here should go home and tell your people to dance it! As for my Oglalas, we intend to continue the ghost dance as long as we please. It matters little to us whether the white people like it or not. . . ."

Old Bear Coat was looking grim, and the Indian hurried on.

"And now, great soldier chief, would you please write down what I have said here and show it to your Great White Father in the East. That is all I have to say."

There was a general commotion throughout the assembly for several minutes, and it seemed discreet to the agency administrators to dismiss the meeting as quickly as possible.

The second of these daring new acts of defiance occurred across the Brulé border. Short Bull had not only recovered his courage completely, but he was stepping up the attack beyond anything which even Kicking Bear had anticipated. He was, in fact, subtly suggesting that he, Short Bull, was now endowed with some of the Messiah's supernatural powers. Leading the ceremonies at Red Leaf's camp, he made a dramatic pronouncement:

"Now listen, my brothers! I have told you before that the day of judgment will come in two seasons. But we are getting so much interference from the whites that I am going to advance the time from what my Father above told me to do, so that the time will be shorter until the Indian is master again! Immediately, starting tomorrow, I am told by my Father above to start ghost-dancing on Pass Creek for one entire moon. . . ."

Pass Creek was about a dozen miles farther west, yet well away from the agency at Pine Ridge, 75 miles farther on. Short Bull knew that he could thus attract villages from both Rosebud and Pine Ridge reservations to this more central location.

"So because the time is so near, my friends," he continued, "I want you all to come there and put your spirit into the dance, and be ready for your dead ones when they return.

"Now you must not be afraid of anything! Some of my relatives have no ears (won't listen) so I will have them blown away. We will dance the rest of this moon, after which the earth will shiver very hard. When that happens, I will start the wind to blowing. We will then see our fathers, mothers, and everybody who has gone before us. We, the Indians, are now living a sacred life!

"Now here is what you must do, my brothers: Even if the soldiers surround you four-deep, those of you on whom I have put holy-shirts will sing a song I have taught you; and then some of the soldiers will drop dead. The rest will start to run, but their horses will sink into the earth. The riders will then jump from their horses, but they, also, will sink into the earth. Then you can do as you desire with them!"

This picture made some of Short Bull's listeners a trifle uneasy, but there was no sound to interrupt him.

"Now know this: All the soldiers and their race will die! My friends and relatives, what I tell you is straight and true. We must gather at Pass Creek where the trees are sprouting. There we will go among our dead relatives. You must not take any earthly things with you. Then the men must take off all of their white men's clothing, and the women must do the same. No one shall be ashamed. Our Father above has told us to do this and we must do as he says.

"Do not be afraid of anything. The guns that you fear

belong to our Father in Heaven, and he will see that they do you no harm. . . . I will now raise my hand up to my Father and close what he has said to you through me. . . ."

Short Bull was beginning to believe that perhaps he really did have the necessary divine power. At any rate, in the ecstasy of the moment he was willing to take the risk of a test if it should come.

Within a week the great ghost dance at Pass Creek was joined by the Brulé bands of Crow Dog, Yellow Thigh and High Hawk. The creek banks were teeming with Indian encampments. About one-third of the Rosebud Brulés were now involved in the dancing in one way or another, if only as observers, and a slightly higher fraction of the Pine Ridge Oglalas. Despite the frantic activity at both Hump's camp and Big Foot's village, only about one in seven of the Cheyenne River Indians were enrolled in ghost dance camps, and at Standing Rock still fewer— about one in ten.

The ghost dancers at Standing Rock were concentrated almost entirely at Sitting Bull's village on the Grand River. In mid-November, Agent McLaughlin decided to go down once more and try to reason with Sitting Bull. But the crafty old medicine man, made bold by the reports of Little Wound's and Short Bull's defiance, was in no mood to knuckle under.

McLaughlin drove up in a light wagon with Louis Primeau, his interpreter, at his side. He stopped the team when he saw the dance circle and whistled softly.

"Great Jehoshaphat!"

There were at least a hundred persons engaged in a furious dance, with a much larger crowd circled around them watching. Groans and wails soared up from the throng through the dance-song. Sitting Bull sat in the door of a tepee at one side of the ring, giving occasional orders. As the visitors watched, a young girl dancer fell to the ground motionless and was carried to Sitting Bull. There she began to mumble weird sounds, and Sitting Bull "interpreted" her wanderings in the other world.

"She has just visited her departed grandmother!" he announced. Then, after bending low over the girl again, "She has seen the Christ! He tells her the Indian will be supreme again!"

A feeling of revulsion swept over McLaughlin, and he motioned Primeau that they should leave quickly before they were noticed. They drove up the river two or three miles to the cabin of Henry Bull Head, one of the agent's police lieutenants, where they talked over the situation and spent the night. Shortly after dawn the next morning the two men returned to the village and came upon Sitting Bull himself as he emerged from his sweat bath, naked except for his breechcloth and moccasins.

McLaughlin and Sitting Bull greeted each other with the customary "*Hau,*" and shook hands. The two wives and some children crowded out of the cabin to see what was going on, and one of the women gave Sitting Bull a shawl for warmth. In less than a minute a crowd of Indians had gathered around them, and McLaughlin decided he had better hurry on with the interview. He tried to draw Sitting Bull to one side, but the crowd moved with them.

"Look here, *Tatanka Iyotanke,*" the agent began, "I

have come to find out what you mean by behaving as you are, in total disregard of the orders given you. Your preaching and practicing this ridiculous Messiah doctrine are causing much uneasiness among the Indians on this reservation, and it needs to be stopped at once."

He nodded to Primeau and the interpreter repeated in Siouan what the agent had said. Then McLaughlin hurried on. He wanted to avoid letting the Indian start an argument.

"You and I have known each other for a long time, and I have done many things to be of service to you over the years. When you sent Bishop Marty to see me from Alberta, in Canada, and you wanted to make peace with the authorities so as to return to your own country after your long exile, did I not move with all my influence to make the arrangements you sought?

"And when you were a prisoner on the Missouri riverboat, being taken from here down to Fort Randall, did I not offer you good advice as to how to conduct yourself so that you ultimately gained your liberty?

"Who was it you wrote to, in a letter carried by Gray Eagle and Little Assiniboine, to get help so that you could return to the Standing Rock reservation? And did I not give you that help?"

McLaughlin continued to pile it on, recollections and anecdotes, for many minutes, reminding the Indian of past favors, large and small.

"And now look at how you return my guardianship!" he said finally. "You are leading your people astray. You are turning them back to primitive times, instead of teaching them to progress. And besides all that, you are making it certain that they will be punished for their misbehavior!"

When this last indictment was translated by Primeau, a loud sneer was emitted by Yellow Otter, standing behind his chief, and the rest of the Indians loosed a roar. But Sitting

Bull turned and ordered them to be quiet. The momentary diversion gave the medicine man a chance to interrupt.

"I tell you I am not deceiving my people," he said coolly. "This new faith is a good thing and it will help Indians everywhere."

"That is rubbish!" snapped McLaughlin. "It will not help them. It will only get them into trouble and you know it!"

A flash of anger crossed the Indian leader's eyes, and there was a moment in which it seemed that he would explode. Then his tight-set jaw relaxed and he said in a quiet voice, "Father, let me make you a proposition that will settle this question. Why do we not go together to the agencies far to the west and beyond the Great Mountains, and talk firsthand to those who know about the Messiah? And we will demand that they take us to him, so we can see him for ourselves. And if they cannot do this, I will return here and tell my people that it is a lie. But if he is truly what they claim, then you can stop bothering our dances."

It was all the agent could do to conceal his contempt for this proposal, but he was tactful.

"Ah, that would be like chasing last year's wind," he said sadly. "But I would like to continue our discussion about it. Why do you not come into the agency and spend a night with me, so that I can persuade you to stop deceiving your people?"

"My heart would like to accept, but I must consult my headmen. If they agree, I may come to the agency on Saturday."

Sitting Bull was plainly dissembling. He had not the slightest intention of falling into McLaughlin's trap.

After shaking hands, McLaughlin picked up the reins and started to pull his wagon away, with Primeau beside him. The crowd around Sitting Bull now loosed sneers and catcalls, but the half-naked medicine man raised his arm and stopped the racket. The agent knew all too well that many of the warriors behind him held their rifles in their hands, and he did not speak or look back as he drove up the hill and over the ridge that put the Indian village out of sight. Then he said, "Louis, I am glad to have that ridge between me and those Winchesters."

They did not know that they had seen their old adversary Sitting Bull alive for the last time.

It required one last dramatic incident at Red Cloud's agency before the Bureau of Indian Affairs gave up and the troops came in. November 11th was ration day, and the village had the appearance of any boisterous cattle town on the day of a festival. The dusty streets were crowded with Indians in shawls and blankets, the women plodding along behind their men with babies on their backs and other children trailing. If the father went into a trading post, the rest of the family sat down out of the traffic and waited.

The agency commissary was jammed with families trying to get their supplies. Ultimately the women would carry their sacks back to their camps, where games and races were going on continuously.

At the corral where government herders were counting

out beef cattle and turning them loose to the heads of each village, in accordance with their listed populations, the warriors galloped after the freed animals and shot them from their ponies. This was the only simulation of the old buffalo hunt left to them, and the Bureau of Indian Affairs was about to call a halt to this practice, labelling it barbaric.

As soon as they were killed, the animals were butchered and dressed in the old way at the nearby camps, and the meat prepared for the trip home.

Into this scene came Lieutenant Thunder Bear and a squad of Indian policemen, under orders from the agent to arrest a swaggering roughneck from No Water's band named Little on a number of offenses.

"Little," announced Thunder Bear, "you are under arrest and must come with me."

The accused man stepped back and drew a butcher knife from his belt. Instantly the crowd of Oglala warriors, almost every one a ghost dancer, swarmed around the policemen with knives bared and their rifles at the ready. Every policeman was seized and his arms pinned behind him.

"Kill them! Kill them!" screamed one of the hotheads.

"Let's burn down the agency!" cried another.

The situation was almost beyond repair when American Horse leaped into the center of the melee and raised his arms.

"Stop this!" he shouted out, and surprisingly the crowd quieted. "What do you think you are doing? Are you going to kill these men of our own race? What will happen then?"

American Horse was snapping his Sioux phrases in contempt. "Are you going to kill these helpless white men here and their women and children, also? And then what do you think will happen? What will these bold deeds of yours lead to? How long do you think you will be able to hold out? Your country here is surrounded with railroads, and thousands of white soldiers will be here within a few days. What ammunition do you have? What provisions do you have? What will become of your women and children when the soldiers attack? Think, think, my brothers! This is child's madness!"

Jack Red Cloud, the old chief's son, plunged forward through the crowd and pushed the barrel of a pistol almost against American Horse's cheek.

"You!" he shrieked angrily. "It is you and your kind who have brought us to this!"

American Horse raised his head slowly away from the pistol and turned his back, walking up the steps of the council building nearby. Without looking back, he closed the door.

Mumbling and cursing, the warriors herded Little away, leaving the Indian police standing helpless and silent.

The next day Agent Royer got an insolent message from Little demanding dismissal of all the policemen who had tried to arrest him, and American Horse moved his family in with the agency doctor for safety's sake.

It was plain enough that the civilian authorities were without influence. Chief Red Cloud was not lifting a finger to quiet things down, but he could have had little influence at this stage anyway.

"Don't you see?" he said to Agent Royer. "We Indians are mocked in our misery. We have no newspapers or other voice to speak for us. We have no redress from the new reductions in our rations. You who eat three times a day, and who see your children well and happy around you, don't understand what these starving Indians feel! We are weak with hunger and maddened by despair. We hold our dying children, and feel their little bodies tremble as their souls go out and leave a dead weight in our hands. Where is there any hope for us on this earth? We feel that God has forgotten us. . . .

"So now men are talking of the son of God, and say that he has come back again. They do not know for sure, and they do not care. They snatch at this hope because it is the only one they have. They scream to him for mercy in their dances, like crazy men. They are only trying to grasp the promises they hear he has made to save them."

Of course even the military commanders in the area were warning Washington that the Indians were under-fed, and that this starvation policy was breeding trouble. But between the indifference of Congress and the clum-siness of the bureaucracy, nothing got done about it as the crisis worsened.

Royer, who saw everything in terms of his own neigh-borhood's peril, fired another telegram to his superiors:

"Indians are dancing in the snow and are wild and crazy. I have fully informed you that employees and government property are at the mercy of these dancers. Why delay by further investigation? We need protection and we need it now. The leaders should be arrested and confined in some military post until the matter is quieted, and this should be done at once."

A few days later, in council with Royer and the local chiefs, American Horse tried once more to appeal to the white man's understanding.

"We were made many promises in the past year," he said quietly, "but have never heard from any of them. The Great Father says if we do what he directs, it will be to our benefit. But instead of this, they are every year cut-ting down our rations and we do not get enough to keep us from suffering. General Crook talked nice to us, and after we signed the (1889) agreement they took our land

and cut down our allowance of food. The commission
made us believe that we would get full sacks if we signed
the treaty, but instead our sacks are empty. . . .

"We are told that if we do as the white man says we will
be better off, but we are getting worse off every year."

Agent Royer had the clerk write this all down when it
was translated, and he sent a copy of it off to the Indian
Affairs office in Washington. But it was too late for
reason. The Commissioner of Indian Affairs had already
conceded that his agents had lost control in the Sioux land.

So on November 17, General Miles ordered Brigadier
General John R. Brooke, commanding the Department of
the Platte, to move troops into the Pine Ridge and
Rosebud reservations. Three days later Brooke marched
into Pine Ridge at the head of three troops of the 9th
Cavalry Regiment, five companies of infantry, a Hotchkiss cannon and a Gatling gun. The 370 soldiers spread
their camp along White Clay Creek.

On the day that General Miles ordered the troops in, the
Indian Commissioner's office asked all agents in Dakota for
their lists of "fomenters of disturbances" who should be arrested and confined. A few days later, Lieutenant Colonel
A. T. Smith arrived on the Rosebud reservation with three
companies of the 8th Infantry and two troops of the 9th
Cavalry—about 200 men—and a Hotchkiss gun.

The arrival of the soldiers set off two opposite
movements among the Indians. Brooke immediately sent
messengers throughout the reservations telling "friendly"
Indians to come into Pine Ridge so that they could be pro-
tected, and hundreds of them hurried to do so. But within
an hour of the arrival of the troops, Little Wound sent
warriors far and wide telling the faithful ghost dancers to
assemble at the mouth of White Clay Creek, 20 miles
northwest of Pine Ridge on the White River.

Several hundreds of Brulés followed the almost senile Two Strike away from the Rosebud agency to a camp on Wounded Knee Creek, and High Hawk and Crow Dog took several hundred more Brulés to Short Bull's ghost dance on Pass Creek. At both places the dance was churning furiously.

A showdown was clearly in the making, and General Miles had no intention of being caught short. In a few days, four more companies of the 2nd Infantry and another troop from the 9th Cavalry arrived at Pine Ridge. Then Colonel James W. Forsyth came in with the entire 7th Cavalry Regiment and a battery of light artillery. Another four companies of infantry reached the Rosebud, and General Brooke announced that he had enlisted 40 Oglala Sioux and 40 Cheyennes as his Indian scout contingent.

Within the western branch of the Sioux nation at this time were some 20,000 persons, of whom 5,000 to 6,000 were potential warriors roughly between the ages of 15 and 50. Even putting the most terrifying face on the ghost-dance threat, there were never at any one time more than about one-fifth of these actively engaged in the ghost-dancing or other resistance to government policy—perhaps 1,200 fighting men. And these were spread in clusters over forty thousand square miles of reservation territory. The highest estimate of organized resistance at any one point was the nearly 3,000 men, women and children in the Bad Lands during the first week of December, of whom probably 750 or 800 were adult warriors.

Against these "hostiles" the United States government had more than 3,000 troops in the field by early December. That the military intended to crush obstreperous behavior by the Indians, once and for all, was plain.

Meanwhile, Agent McLaughlin, in his rather remote bailiwick far to the north, had no need for extra troops because

Fort Yates was right next door. What he wanted was to get the person of Sitting Bull out of the Standing Rock reservation. The medicine man alone, he felt, was responsible for whatever rebellion there was among the Hunkpapa band.

McLaughlin had the full cooperation of a number of long-standing Indian leaders under his charge—Chief Gall, who 14 years earlier participated in the assault that destroyed Custer on the Little Big Horn; John Grass, whose village on the Missouri River was a center of opposition to the ghost dance from the beginning; and several others.

Sitting Bull was the poisoning influence. With his removal, the agent was confident the situation would become calm and manageable.

Nevertheless, now that the Indian office was finally persuaded to arrest the man, McLaughlin had to ask the authorities to hold off a little longer for strategic reasons. The Dakota weather had remained unseasonably mild. With a little nip of winter which surely must come any day now, he suggested, the ghost-dance crowd would tend to disperse and stay indoors. Thus it would be less likely that the Indian police would have a mob to contend with when they went to make the arrest.

McLaughlin's superiors saw the logic in this and acceded to the recommendation.

On the theory that there was strength in union, Chief Big Foot decided early in November to move his village back closer to Hump's camp, 25 miles down the Cheyenne River. The band's rations were now being issued nearby at Cherry Creek anyway. Now the ghost dance was going near both camps, day and night.

The Horn Clouds and Yellow Hawks had been hunting antelope for more than a month on the Little Missouri River near the Dog Teeth Buttes. They had gone properly to Captain Henissee and obtained a pass to travel. Upon returning with a supply of meat, they got the last of their hay stacked and the cabins chinked for the winter, so despite their disinterest in the ghost dance they decided to go along on the excursion downriver.

Big Foot kept his people near Hump's village for a month before the military started closing in on him and he suffered a shattering disillusionment at the hands of Hump. Toward the end of the month, Agent Palmer made his final visit to these boiling ghost dances, and he was much concerned—partly because across the river in the new "white territory" taken from the Sioux there was now a village of eighteen or twenty frightened home-steaders for whose safety he was indirectly responsible.

The agent's Indian staff worked hard on Hump, ap-pealing to his vanity to persuade him that a great future awaited him as a police officer and scout. Hump had en-joyed his prestige in these roles, and was plainly wavering. This naturally disturbed Big Foot, and he called a council.

"My brothers," he said to his headmen, "I do not know what is going to happen here. There are dangers all around us. Some of them lie within the hearts of our own people. If we are ever to force the whites to treat us justly, it will not be through bowing too meekly and accepting their bribes, but rather through standing firm and insisting on our rights as Wakan-tanka's children.

"Now word has come to me that armies of white soldiers have arrived at Red Cloud's agency and also among the Brulés. I fear that we may be next. I do not know where the danger will break out, or what course we may have to take to protect ourselves. But I propose that we of our band all stay together in one village now, and that each warrior gather whatever guns and ammunition he can and preserve them against any crisis."

The danger from Hump was precisely what Big Foot had begun to suspect. But it was going to take some doing to get his defection, and General Miles felt that he had the perfect solution. He had thought long and hard about each of the principal ghost-dance leaders—Sitting Bull, Hump, Big Foot, Little Wound, and so on—and about what Achilles' heel each one might have that could be pricked to break down their solidarity.

In Hump's case, the answer was obvious. After the defeats of Custer and Crook in the Powder River country back in 1876, Hump had such an undisputed place as a war chief among the Teton Sioux that no amount of subsequent ambivalence toward the white man could alter it. When he brought his people in surrender during the mass capitulation of 1877, he characteristically became a dedicated scout for Bear Coat Miles, then a colonel. In the very summer of Hump's surrender, Chief Joseph's Nez Percé were being chased in and out of the mountains from Oregon to the Yellowstone, through the Bitterroot Range and high into Montana, their secluded camps being shot up time and again, their leaders slain one after the other, and sometimes their helpless women and children shot and clubbed to death as well.

Late that fall, when Chief Joseph and the remnants of his band were cornered in northern Montana, Colonel

Miles was ordered to the scene from Fort Keogh on the Yellowstone to help with the capture. Hump, his faithful scout, led Miles' 600 mounted troops across country to the Bear Paw Mountains where Chief Joseph was trapped. The fighting had been bloody and the little band of Nez Percé was being decimated day after day. Finally, assured by Miles that he and the general in command, Oliver O. Howard, would try to see that they were returned to their home neighborhood, Chief Joseph surrendered, and Hump heard the speech that he made to his captors:

"Tell General Howard I know his heart. What he told me before I have in my heart. I am tired of fighting. Our chiefs are killed. Looking Glass is dead. Toohoolhoolzote is dead. The old men are all dead; it is the young men who say yes and no. He who led the young men (Chief Ollikut) is dead. It is cold and we have no blankets. The little children are freezing to death. I want to have time to look for my children and see how many I can find. Maybe I shall find them dead. Hear me, my chiefs: I am tired. My heart is sick and sad. From where the sun now stands, I will fight no more forever."

As a matter of fact, instead of being returned to their own country, the Nez Percé band was sent to a swampy area along the Missouri River near Fort Leavenworth, Kansas, where within a few months one-fourth of them died of malaria and pneumonia.

Colonel Miles was made a brigadier general in 1880, and he kept his friend and scout, Hump, with him for a total of seven years under the judicious eye of a smart young officer, Captain Ezra Ewers. Hump and Ewers hit it off at once, and formed a fast friendship.

Finally Miles thought it time to pay off Hump for his services, and he persuaded the Indian Affairs office to make him chief of police on his home reservation along the Cheyenne River. Even when Hump bitterly resisted the Crook treaty commission in 1889, no one quite dared to threaten his position as police chief.

On the same day that Agent Palmer made his last visit to the Cheyenne River ghost dance camps and Chief Big Foot began to have misgivings about Hump's fidelity, General Miles fired off a wire to the Army's Department of Texas, asking for the loan of Captain Ewers. Why not have Ewers go to work on his old friend Hump, thought Miles.

The captain started north by train the same day and arrived in the new South Dakota capital of Pierre, on the Missouri River, six days later. There he found waiting for him General Miles' orders on how to proceed, and he went on across the river to talk to the officers at Fort Bennett and to Agent Palmer from the nearby agency.

Palmer warned that the ghost dancers were wild and well-armed. "Captain, you wouldn't believe what I saw out there less than a week ago—mad fanaticism, absolutely savage. The sight of a uniform may be even worse. I suggest you trot a good-sized troop along behind you."

Ewers had been looking over the young officers around him.

"Thank you, Mr. Palmer," he smiled. And then turning to Lieutenant Harry C. Hale, he said, "Say, Lieutenant, they tell me you've been back and forth to the Camp of Observation several times. . . ."

"That's right, sir."

"Can you go with me at daybreak or earlier, and show me the way?"

"Certainly, Captain. How many men will you want?"

"I'll discuss that with you in a few minutes," said Ewers, and he turned to shake hands with the group and say goodnight to Agent Palmer.

"I need a lot of sleep," he said pleasantly.

When the others had gone, he turned back to Hale. "I want you and me to go alone, Lieutenant. Do you have any qualms?"

"If you say so, not in the least, sir."

"All right, let's get some rest." And they shook hands.

The next morning early they were trotting briskly on the road to Cherry Creek, 50 miles up the river, where they arrived in late afternoon. Hump was off in the hills somewhere, but a runner was dispatched to find him.

Narcisse Narcelle, the agency farmer, happened to be at the village, and the two officers had a long visit with him about the current situation. Narcelle, a French-Indian, had a demonstration ranch in the southwest corner of the reservation. It was the agency farmer's job to teach the Indians farming methods, but Narcelle had found it necessary for weeks to spend his whole time trying to dissuade the Minneconjous from their incessant ghost-dancing. He had no special competency or knowledge about farming anyway; few of the agency farmers did.

Just at dusk Hump came riding in, and the two old friends put on a demonstration that could only be called affectionate. Ewers found his assignment a ridiculously easy one.

"Hump, my brother," he began at last, "old Bear Coat sent me to find you."

Hump beamed. How was his old friend, General Miles, he wanted to know. The conversation rolled along relaxed and easy. It became apparent, long before the business at hand was reached, that Hump was in a mood for something new, some change of interest. He was sated with ghost-dancing. He could not see that it was leading to anything profitable.

Finally Ewers got to it.

"General Miles sent me to tell you personally that he would like to have you bring your people into Fort Bennett. Some Sioux and Cheyennes are causing some trouble, and Bear Coat does not want his old friend Hump to get involved in it and get hurt. He wants to protect your people, and he thinks this can best be assured if they will live down near the agency for a while."

Hump ruminated for several minutes, and he was not just being coy. He was thinking of the risks and of his status as an Indian leader. But finally he said, "If this is what General Miles wishes, this is what Hump and his Minneconjous will do."

Within an hour, the word had spread up and down the Cheyenne River bottom and families were beginning to load up their wagons and travois preparatory to a morning departure. Only a hard core of ghost dancers, perhaps ten per cent, brooded in their lodges and declined to put themselves under the muzzles of the white soldiers' guns at Fort Bennett.

The long caravan started eastward down the agency road the next forenoon, and three days later—on December 9—the Hump band was encamped in a sprawling village close by the Cheyenne River agency on the Missouri.

The effect of these events upon Big Foot was severely demoralizing. He was forced to acknowledge that the power of the ghost dance to hold Indians to the faith was indeed limited, even illusory. As a result, his own commitment now entered upon a phase of gradual disenchantment. The spiritual uplift which he had enjoyed at the moment of uniting with Hump in a common crusade suffered a doubly devastating collapse. Hump's defection left Big Foot helpless and alone on the Cheyenne river, encircled by threats against which he had no sure defense.

Adding to this tension and pressure, word had come only the day before that a new commander was now at Henissee's camp, a few miles from Big Foot's home village, with a total of some 200 soldiers and two of the dread Hotchkiss or, as the Dakotas called them, "shoot-twice" guns.

The new commanding officer was Lieutenant Colonel Edwin V. Sumner. Big Foot decided that he had better get back and hear what this soldier chief in his front yard had to say, whether good or bad. So as soon as Hump's people had cleared out, he called a council and suggested that they go home to Deep Creek.

And the next day, December 7, they did.

CHAPTER III

THE SOLDIERS

General Brooke's policy, when the troops came to Pine Ridge on November 20, of offering asylum and plenty of food to all "friendly" Indians who came into the agency had borne fruit from the beginning. His Indian scouts—No Neck, Woman's Dress, and others—roamed along White Clay Creek to the White River and beyond, mixing with the disgruntled and urging the leaders that much was to be gained by returning to the agency while an amnesty lasted. The mixed-blood scouts and interpreters were also effective in this proselyting—the three Shangreau brothers, Baptiste (Big Bat) Pourier, Little Bat Garnier, Frank Grouard, and others.

Little Wound, for example, whose rallying cry to the ghost dancers on the day the troops arrived had brought nearly 2,000 Indians to his camp at the mouth of the White Clay, soon found the confusion more than he could stomach. In exactly one week, he came marching back to the agency with his whole band trooping along behind, and asked the military where he could camp.

Within a few hours Big Road and No Water and their bands followed. Since other groups of Indians from all over the Pine Ridge and Rosebud reservations had been flowing in during the week, the knolls along the creek banks for miles were covered with Indian camps. The "village" of Pine Ridge now contained some 4,000 Indians and about 1,000 soldiers.

General Brooke tried to keep Indians who had not yet repudiated the ghost dance separated from the community of "friendlies," but the distinction wasn't always easy.

Meanwhile, Short Bull's huge camp of ghost dancers on

Pass Creek was becoming a problem for him. He saw that some new stimulation was required or the bands would begin drifting away to the agency where so many of their relatives and friends had gone. So he decided to make a long march up the White River and join the dancing at Little Wound's camp on the White Clay.

It took this caravan nearly a week to travel the 90 or more miles, and it arrived at the destination only to learn that Little Wound, No Water and Big Road and their followers had already gone back to the agency. This was only the first of a series of frustrations that were about to befall Short Bull and his companion Kicking Bear. For Kicking Bear was also there with his own band of ghost dancers, sullen and dejected over the defection of the three powerful Oglala leaders.

"And there is still more disturbing news," said Kicking Bear. "While you have been traveling to this place, the horse soldiers of the company that Custer led at Little Big Horn have arrived at the agency."

At the battle 14 years earlier, the Sioux and Cheyennes didn't even know who it was they had killed, but they had heard plenty about it in the years since, of course.

Short Bull got the significance of this news at once. A lust for revenge was no mystery to the Indian, and he assumed that Custer's military heirs felt it as well.

Not only had the 7th Cavalry Regiment come into Pine Ridge, but also additional companies of infantry and other troops. A larger troop of Oglala scouts and one of Cheyennes had now been organized, about 150 men altogether, and they were ready to go to work for the Army.

"I think we need to put more distance between us and the white soldiers," said Short Bull after a few minutes' thought. "It is too easy for the agent's spies to get at our people here. Also, it is too easy for the timid ones to decide to knock down their tepees and go running into the commissary for food and clothing."

Kicking Bear had been thinking the same thing.

"What you say is right. If there is truth in the Messiah's promise, we need to find a place where we can protect ourselves until spring when it will be fulfilled. We could get enough food for our people through raids on the agency's beef herd, or from the herds of ranchers. But the problem is finding a hiding place from which we can hold off the soldiers despite their murderous cannons."

"Hau! I was thinking about this as we came up the river, the other day. Right across from the mouth of Porcupine Creek there is that high table—but it is not very good because it has sloping sides which the horse soldiers could ascend. . . ."

Kicking Bear was beginning to see some light. "There is the big table opposite Wounded Knee Creek, but the soldiers could climb that one in many places, too."

The two men were visualizing the vast stretch of Bad Lands which begins north of the Bad River, a tributary of the Missouri, and sweeps southwestward for a hundred miles toward the Nebraska border. The bed of some prehistoric sea, several hundred feet of this soil had been washed out as the waters drained away over the aeons. Then the area was eroded by wind and rain for countless further centuries until today it is mostly hard clay without nutrients to support more than occasional desert vegetation.

In the eroding process, a few areas harder or rockier than the rest stood their ground, held a few inches of grass-growing soil on their tabletops, and became raised fastnesses whose sides sometimes dropped precipitously 300 feet or more to the Bad Lands floor.

Such a tabletop near the White River was the one to which Short Bull had referred, later to be called Stirk

Table. It is small, relatively—perhaps a couple of miles each way across its top. And it is softer than some, so that its eroded sides are more gently sloping.

The "big one" mentioned by Kicking Bear was Cuny Table, a plateau 14 miles long and averaging three or four miles in width. There were innumerable places where Cuny could be ascended, and the rebellious Indians didn't begin to have enough manpower to guard its 50 miles of circumference anyway.

The Teton Sioux knew this territory well enough; they had been in and out of it many times, but there had never been any great incentive to hover in the vicinity. Animal life was scarce in this barren region, so it was not good for hunting except on rare occasions when some deer or elk could be trapped on one of its tables. And there was little water to support human life except in the muddy streams at the Bad Lands floor. So the Dakotas knew that the area was an unmerciful oven in the summertime and a place where drifting snow might conceal treacherous gullies in midwinter. For the most part they stayed away from it.

There was also Red Shirt's Table, his former village at the north end of it overlooking the Cheyenne River, but that table also was easily accessible and impossible to defend. (Red Shirt had long since taken his people into the agency to keep out of trouble.)

And there was Sheep Mountain Table farther north, in the worst part of the Bad Lands—a rocky, miserable place to try to take wagons and women and children, let alone beef herds.

"Now, my brothers," said Short Bull at last, "I am thinking of that point, that island, at the north side of the big table—it is part of the big table (Cuny) only it is not part of it. If we were on top of that point, we would not even have to defend the sharp saddle connecting it with the larger table, because no man can cross it. We would need only to defend the two or three steep deer trails up its sides. The bluecoats could never get their horses and guns up those trails if we were defending them."

Fortunately, this strategy of Short Bull's was never put to a test, for the Army could have lobbed its Hotchkiss shells from Cuny Table and blown every living thing off the top of the little annex. To Short Bull and Kicking Bear, however, it seemed they had landed on a near-perfect solution. The detached segment of Cuny Table became known to all Americans within a week as "the Stronghold," so identified by General Brooke and the nation's military leaders, and therefore by the dozens of newspaper and magazine correspondents who had swarmed to Pine Ridge for this showdown with the Sioux Indians.

The Stronghold was about two miles long and a mile wide. There was a substantial cover of buffalo grass on its top which would support the necessary livestock through the winter. The critical job was to find the beef supply and get it up there, and that required some careful planning.

Early the next morning, Short Bull and Kicking Bear sent messengers throughout the ghost dance camps to call the headmen into a general council. When it convened, they began immediately assigning responsibilities to the chiefs, one to gather the necessary scouts, another the hunters to plan the cattle thefts, another the dog soldiers who would police the march down the river, and so on.

So on November 30, only a few days after the two prophets had led their flocks into Little Wound's erstwhile camp, they were leading them out again—this time running for a refuge which they believed the white soldiers could not successfully attack. In their company still were such chiefs and other leaders as Torn Belly, at whose ghost dance Agent Gallagher had had his narrow escape two months earlier; Jack Red Cloud, belligerent son of the old chief; Turning Bear and High Hawk and Crow Dog, the Brulés; White Horse and Eagle Pipe and No Flesh and a half dozen more.

The day before they left for the Stronghold, Short Bull and Crow Dog sent runners to the camp on Wounded Knee Creek where the fuzzy-headed Two Strike now held sway. The messengers asked Two Strike's headmen to join the hegira, and they agreed enthusiastically. There were several hundred Wazhazha Brulés, all of Two Strike's band, Good Thunder of the Wovoka pilgrimage who now had a ghost dance crowd of his own, and five or six lesser chiefs with their people—more than 200 lodges altogether. Their instructions were to meet the throng of Kicking Bear's and Short Bull's followers across the White River, at the approach to Cuny Table, in two days. And this they did.

Numerous "friendly" Indians along Wounded Knee and Grass Creeks, worried by the belligerence of Two Strike's dancers, had fled to the agency earlier at General Brooke's invitation, leaving their cabins and farms unguarded. So as Two Strike's horde swarmed across country to meet Short Bull, it picked up all the stray cattle in sight, plundered the cabins of anything valuable, and frequently burned the haystacks just as a rebuke to backsliders who had run to the whites for protection.

Short Bull's hunters, meanwhile, had discovered the location of the agency beef herd across the river from the mouth of Willow Creek, almost directly in their path. As soon as the procession of marchers, travois, wagons and pony herds had cleared the area and was nearing the slope to Cuny Table, eight or ten miles downriver, the hunting parties cut into the cattle herds and swept out several hundred animals with them. The agency's chief herder and his men were helpless, of course, and they managed to keep out of the marauders' way.

The Stronghold now had its beef supply.

General Brooke wisely did not allow himself to be thrown into a panic by any of these developments. He was relieved, in fact, when he discovered that the fugitives were settling down in the Bad Lands instead of attempting some foolhardy dash for Canada or other far parts. This kept them well within his reach, and he immediately began sending parties of "friendly" Indians up to the Stronghold to parley. Most of them got themselves fired upon, however, and returned to the agency chastened.

Then Brooke learned that Father John Jutz, who ran the Holy Rosary Mission School north of town, was much trusted by the Indian rebels, and had even been promised by them that his mission would not be harmed in case of fighting. The general asked Jutz if he would not go to the Stronghold and try to talk with the Indians there.

The priest agreed at once. He looked around the agency for someone to accompany him and found, surprisingly enough, one of the ghost dance leaders who had suddenly decided to come home—Jack Red Cloud. The two set out about noon on December 3, and at suppertime they were ready to ascend the table. But they were held up by out-lying pickets until late at night, when word finally came to let them pass.

By midnight, Jutz was deep in debate with the Indian leaders, and the council continued until daybreak. For a man of great compassion like the priest, it was a night of anguish. The fugitives poured out their grievances, one after the other. The complaints were altogether justified, on the whole, yet Father Jutz had no authority to promise remedies of any kind.

Most of the Indians at the Stronghold were Brulés, and the Brulés had been treated with special shabbiness by the American government on a number of occasions.

"My friend Black Robe," said Two Strike, "do you know

what they did to us at Rosebud? A man came from the Great Father and pretended to count us, only he couldn't find two thousand of our people so he cut the beef ration by two cattle out of every seven, when we were already hungry. Even our good agent told him he was wrong, and they sent our agent away—maybe to jail, I don't know."

Chief Lip of the Wazhazhas repeated a speech that he had made to agents several times in the past year without result.

"Yes, we were once Brulés, but we have been living with the Oglalas for nearly two generations and we wish to stay with them. Why, then, does the Great Father insist on putting us back with the Rosebud people when we wish to live among our Oglala brothers?"

The bureaucrats had been unable to come to grips with this simple problem, and the outraged Wazhazhas had marched over to Wounded Knee Creek on their own. So they were, in a sense, outlaws.

Father Jutz simply listened and looked sad.

"And another thing," stormed Eagle Pipe, "you tell us to walk into the agency and surrender, but we are not fools and we know that most of us are now on a list of chiefs and headmen who are to be arrested. Do you think we are going to be locked in the soldiers' big iron house and then dance with joy? No, we would rather die fighting for what is just and honest!"

At last they all ran out of oratory, and the priest took advantage of a momentary silence.

"My friends, it is getting light in the East. I know there is much justice on your side. I can only beg you not to stop listening to what the soldier chief wants to say to you. If you would only pick a few to go back with me, I myself, whom you trust, will guarantee your safety. I want you to talk to General Brooke. He is an honorable man. I will send word ahead that you must come with completely free passage in and out of the agency."

The men put their heads together, and the alacrity with which they accepted Father Jutz' proposition was evidence of their anxiety to find a solution for this agonizing conflict.

They promptly appointed an escort of two-dozen armed warriors and a delegation of headmen consisting of Two Strike, who was senior, Turning Bear, Big Turkey, High Pine, Big Bad Horse, and Bull Dog.

There were a few who had no intention of risking arrest by going along—principally Kicking Bear, Crow Dog and Short Bull. Even some members of the delegation itself had little confidence that Jutz could prevent a trick on the part of the white soldiers. They therefore ordered their warrior escorts to swab themselves with war paint and be ready for battle.

Bedecked in eagle feathers and other war trappings, the cavalcade marched down off the Stronghold table and headed across country toward the White River and the agency. By sunset they were at Father Jutz' mission, four miles from Pine Ridge, and here they spent the night, keeping ample guards on watch.

When daylight came again, some of the bellicosity had gone out of the group and they decided to omit the war paint and eagle feathers. Actually they were getting more apprehensive by the minute about the weakness of their position.

Two Strike had a white cloth mounted on a pole as they started the last lap into Pine Ridge, and he decided to ride in the buggy with Father Jutz for security reasons. Once or twice, at the crack of a hunter's rifle in the distance, the warriors almost bolted. But the priest's reassuring voice held them together and, despite several dead stops, the procession finally crept into the agency. There the warriors turned their ponies into two files protecting the delegation as it marched into Brooke's headquarters.

Now all the speeches that had been made to Jutz were repeated to the general and two colonels, Frank Wheaton and James Forsyth, who sat at his side.

Brooke was in a good humor. "Of course there are grievances," he declared amiably. "These can all be straightened out if the leaders will only bring their people down from the Stronghold and settle at the agency. The Great Father wants you to do this so we can solve our problems face to face, rather than through irresponsible parties.

"I tell you honestly, I am going to see that your people get plenty of food down here. They shouldn't be permitted to go hungry any longer. And another thing: I need a lot of your young men as scouts. I want to hire them. The soldiers didn't come here to fight, but only to protect the settlers and keep the peace."

When this was translated to the delegation, Turning Bear arose and announced that he had something to say.

"Mr. Interpreter, would you please say to the great soldier chief that it is a puzzle to us why you need our men as scouts if we are all such good friends and there is no enemy. But if you wish to pay our young men for scouting even when there is no enemy and no war, I suppose we should be happy to be paid for doing nothing."

The other Indians laughed uneasily at the joke.

"Now we have talked among ourselves through many councils," Turning Bear continued, "about this matter of coming into the agency. For one thing, you now have collected about a thousand Indian lodges or more along this valley, and their livestock has already eaten up all the grass around here, so I don't know how we could feed our ponies. . . ."

Turning Bear hesitated a moment. He was going to say something about the freedom of the ghost dancers, and then decided against it.

"For another thing, it would take us a long time to get all of our people down from the Stronghold table. The old men and women have no ponies to ride, and there aren't enough horses to pull the wagons in which these people might ride. You would have to send horses and wagons for them, and also bring back our large beef herd. . . ."

He didn't mention where the cattle had come from.

"So we will have to think carefully about all that. However," and now he turned directly to the interpreter again, "you might tell the soldier chief that it would help matters if we all had a good meal before we have to start the long trip back to the Stronghold to talk this matter over!"

There was a general mumble of agreement from the delegation, and when Brooke heard the translation he immediately sent orders for a feast to be prepared at the warehouse nearby.

The Indians ate ravenously, and then watched a squaw dance which General Brooke thought would climax the softening-up process. The commander deluded himself that everything was settled, and he wired General Miles in Washington that the Stronghold Indians would all be coming in shortly.

But Miles read the press dispatches about the feast and the squaw dance, and he wasn't impressed. In place of congratulations, he shot back a couple of acid reprimands about consorting with the rebels instead of demanding restitution for their misconduct.

While that telegraphic exchange was going on, Two Strike and his delegation were trotting along on their day's journey back to the Stronghold. Louis Shangreau, French-Indian scout, was tagging along close behind with

No Neck and thirty of Brooke's "friendly" Indians, who were intended to bolster the talk of surrender.

When the party arrived at the rebels' camp, it found a full-scale ghost dance in progress, and Short Bull had no intention of quieting it down. The dance went on all the next day and the following night, and then, having made his point, Short Bull stopped it and allowed Two Strike to call a council of the leaders. Members of the delegation and even some of the "friendly" Indians spoke, one after another. Ultimately Louis Shangreau found an opportunity to address the group.

"Your delegates have told you what the white soldier chief had to say. My orders are merely to tell you that the agent would forgive you all if you would return now. He promises you more rations, also. But he must warn you that the ghost dance will not be permitted to continue."

General Brooke would have been surprised to see Two Strike arise and announce bluntly that, in that case, he was opposed to surrender. Crow Dog concurred. Then Short Bull, now the spiritual leader of this whole assemblage, stood up and assumed a dramatic pose.

"I have arisen to say something of great importance! My friends, you have heard the words of our brothers who came from the agency camps. I have weighed their words carefully, as I am sure you have. If the Great Father would permit us to continue the dance, if he would give us more rations, and if he would quit taking away portions of our reservation all the time, then I would be in favor of returning to the agency."

Now he turned directly to Shangreau and his voice grew sharp.

"But even if you say he will, how do we know whether you are telling the truth? We have been lied to so many times that we do not believe any words the agent sends to us. If we return, he will only take away our guns and ponies, and then he will put some of us in jail for stealing cattle and robbing the ranch houses."

Short Bull was no fool. It was precisely this failure to punish the culprits for which General Miles had scorched Brooke by telegram, a couple of days earlier.

"So we prefer to stay here and die, if necessary, rather than lose our liberty. Here we are free, and we have plenty of beef. We can dance all the time in obedience to the command of Wakan-tanka. I tell you to go back to your agent and tell him the Lakotas in the Bad Lands are not coming in!"

There was a yell of approval from the warriors. They swarmed out into the dance circle and began again. This time the dance went on without interruption for two days.

Shangreau and his companions stayed at one side and watched, talking quietly to one warrior and then another. Among those with whom the scout pleaded most forcefully were Crow Dog and Two Strike.

It was the afternoon of December 10 when Two Strike, indifferently watching the tired ghost dancers, suddenly got to his feet and announced to the chiefs and headmen around him that he was taking his 140 or more lodges to Pine Ridge. The effect was electric. The warriors stood speechless, as if asking each other whether to cheer or draw their knives for battle.

In this gap of a few seconds, Crow Dog likewise arose and said, "I agree. It is time to give up this game and surrender."

Short Bull leapt to his feet facing the crowd and crouched as if frozen. There was fury in his face and in his voice when he spoke.

"What kind of brothers are these?" he snarled. "This is a time when we must all stand together. Do not leave! Stay and help your brothers! These men from the agency are liars. They will lead you back there and have you thrown into jail. Louis here is at the bottom of this—"

He thrust his pointing finger into the scout's face and then turned to his own headmen.

"This man is a traitor!" he screamed. "*Kill him! Kill him!*"

Some of the warriors seized their rifles by the muzzles and ran at Shangreau to club him down, but his agency companions moved quickly to his defense, supported by Two Strike's headmen. For the next few minutes there were heads being split right and left, several men were stabbed, and a few shot. Those who could reach their ponies rode into the melee shooting bows and arrows, firing pistols, or swinging sticks and clubs. There soon were a dozen or more men on the ground, several badly wounded.

Some said afterward that Crow Dog's histrionics stopped the mayhem, but the truth is that—as in any family brawl—the anger of the crowd began to subside as quickly as it had arisen. Almost at the same moment, everyone noticed Crow Dog's figure seated on the ground with his blanket pulled over his head in shame. In a short time, all was quiet again except for the groans of the injured.

Crow Dog lifted off his covering. "Is it fitting," he called out, "that brothers in the Lakota family should kill each other? I myself am going to White Clay (the agency). Kill me if you want to, right now, and prevent me from starting."

After a short silence, he concluded, "I believe the agent's words are true, and it is better to return than to stay here any longer. I am not afraid to die!"

Short Bull saw that he was defeated, and he moved to one side. In an hour most of the camp was loaded up for travel, and by late afternoon a long, straggling caravan was winding its way down from the Stronghold along the narrow paths to the Bad Lands floor. The clay soil was frozen but there was no snow here yet.

Louis Shangreau and his agency "friendlies" rode along easily on the flanks. They were only four miles down the road toward the White River when a commotion caused them to look backward. There, sure enough, came the Kicking Bear and Short Bull bands down the slope, following the parade.

Shangreau kept moving and pretended not to notice. But his strategy did not quite succeed. After a few miles the prophets got to thinking again about the jail that unquestionably awaited them, and they called on their followers to turn back to the Stronghold. A couple of hundred of the faithful reversed themselves once more and returned to the high table with the ghost dance leaders.

Fortunately, all the rest of the weary travelers managed to reach Pine Ridge by December 15, the day Sitting Bull was killed 200 miles to the north. If word of that event had come earlier, it might have blighted General Brooke's coup irretrievably.

What happened that morning on the Grand River was going to throw Chief Big Foot's plans into confusion once more. The echo of distant events was already hounding him; now he would be accused of complicity even though his part in the drama was quite innocent and accidental.

Agent McLaughlin, along with the other Sioux agents, had received on December 1 the order to obey and cooperate with the military forces in the area. The Standing Rock agent already had a good relationship with the 8th Cavalry at Fort Yates nearby, and when the order for Sitting Bull's arrest finally arrived on December 12, McLaughlin discussed it thoroughly with Lieutenant Colonel William F. Drum and his officers at the fort.

McLaughlin's Indian police had been keeping a close watch on Sitting Bull's operations. Colonel Drum had great confidence in the experienced agent and therefore in his Indian police also. It was decided between them that the arrest of Sitting Bull should be made on the twentieth, since most of the Indians would be at the agency that day picking up their monthly rations, instead of at home around the ghost dance circle.

Sitting Bull did not know of the order for his arrest. He had received at almost the same time an invitation from Kicking Bear and Short Bull to visit them at the Stronghold. The temptation was almost irresistible, but Sitting Bull hardly knew how to get away. The agent's spies were everywhere. He concluded that he must take the offensive, therefore, and he sent one of his headmen, Bull Ghost, to McLaughlin with a letter written by Sitting Bull's somewhat educated son-in-law, Andrew Fox. It was mostly illiterate and the agent could scarcely make head or tail of some of it, but this much he did decipher:

"I meeting with all my Indians today & writing to you this order. God made . . . the white race & also the Red race . . . but the white high(er) than the Indians. . . . I wish no one to come to me in my pray(ers) with guns or knife. . . . And you, my friend, today you thing I am foll (fool). . . . So you don't like me. My Friend, I don't like

my self when some one is foll. . . . (You think) if I am not
here, then the Indians will be civilization. . . . I will let you
know something: I got to go to Agency (Pine Ridge) & to
know this pray (religion). So I let you know that, & the
Police man told me you going to take all our Poneys, guns
too. So I want you let me know. . . . I want answer back
soon.   Sitting Bull."

McLaughlin hurriedly sent the policeman White Bird off
to Lieutenant Bull Head, down the Grand River, to warn
him that Sitting Bull might try to flee at any moment.

"If he should (attempt to leave), *you must stop him.*"
were McLaughlin's specific words. "If he does not listen to
you, do as you see fit. Use your own discretion in the matter and it will be all right!" No officer of the law ever had
a clearer *carte blanche* than that.

McLaughlin then added orders to Bull Head to gather
all of the Indian police within call at the road crossing of
Oak Creek, midway between the agency and Sitting Bull's
village, on the pretext of starting to build a halfway
shelter there. The logs had already been hauled in a few
days before. The agent also sent fifteen of his own police
to Oak Creek to join the others in beginning the work, so
they would be close by.

As a further backup measure, McLaughlin sent Sergeant
Shave Head to tell Bull Head verbally that Sitting Bull
was to be stopped from escaping "by whatever means are
necessary."

Sitting Bull was correct in his suspicion that Lieutenant
Bull Head had many eyes working for him. The policeman then reported critical news to the white school-
teacher, John Carignan, who wrote down matters of importance and sent the reports to the agency regularly.
So when, on December 13, Bull Head discovered several

extra ponies in Sitting Bull's corral and recognized that the medicine man was preparing to make a break, he promptly got the news to Carignan. The next day Policeman Hawk Man raced the 40 miles in a little over four hours to carry the message to McLaughlin.

"Sitting Bull has received a letter from the Pine Ridge outfit," said Carignan's note, "asking him to come over there as God was about to appear. Sitting Bull's people want him to go, but he has sent a letter to you asking your permission, and if you do not give it he is going to go anyway. He has been fitting up his horses to stand a long ride, and will go horseback in case he is pursued. Bull Head would like to arrest him at once, before he has a chance of giving them the slip. He thinks that if Sitting Bull gets the start, it will be impossible to catch him."

The letter went on to say that Sitting Bull's council had decided to have him leave on the 15th—the very next morning! That gave the agent and Colonel Drum only a few hours. Immediately they drafted orders for Lieutenant Bull Head:

"I believe that the time has arrived for the arrest of Sitting Bull, and that it can be made by the Indian police without much risk. . . ." A presumptuous statement, but flattering to Bull Head!

"I therefore desire you to make the arrest before daylight tomorrow morning, and try to get back to the Sitting Bull Road crossing at Oak Creek by daylight or as soon thereafter as possible. The cavalry will leave tonight and reach Oak Creek before daylight tomorrow morning, where they will remain until they hear from you. . . . I have ordered all the police at Oak Creek to proceed to Carignan's school and await your orders. This gives you a force of 42 policemen for the arrest."

After his signature, the agent added once more:

"P.S.—You must not let him escape under any circumstances."

Sergeant Red Tomahawk galloped westward at sundown with two copies of this order, one in English and one in Santee Sioux, and another rider bore a copy of the instructions to Carignan.

Captain E. G. Fechet and a hundred soldiers left Fort Yates at midnight for Oak Creek, hauling a Hotchkiss gun.

Sitting Bull's headmen had been maintaining a substantial guard around his cabins most of the time, but on this occasion the ghost dance had continued until early evening and everyone was exhausted. The night air was now getting bitterly cold, and most of the men had gone to their homes and fallen into a sound sleep.

Just before daybreak Bull Head's police moved noiselessly through the still camp and surrounded both of Sitting Bull's cabins. The lieutenant himself walked into the Hunkpapa leader's bedroom and said quietly, "Come, father, I am ordered to take you into the agency."

Sitting Bull sat up and rubbed his eyes.

"What's going on here?" he asked, genuinely puzzled.

Pretty Plume, one of his wives, began to wail.

"Now let's not make any trouble, father," said Bull Head. "Just get dressed and come along sensibly."

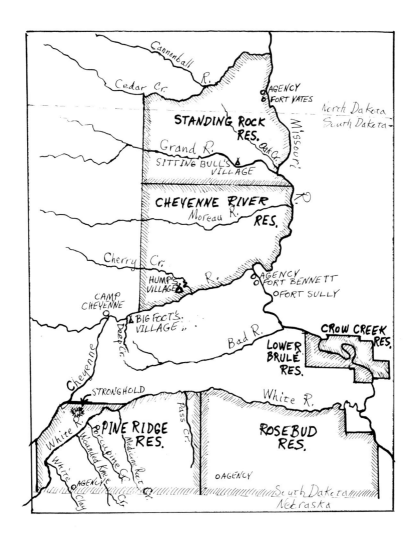

Sioux Reservations — 1890

One of the Indian leaders in a group at Washington in 1888, identified as Spotted Elk, later known as Big Foot. However, there is nothing else to authenticate the identification.

The frozen body of Big Foot after the blizzard.

Smithsonian Institution Photo

View of Big Foot's camp after the battle.

Collecting the dead for burial two days after the battle.

Monument to Sitting Bull near Mobridge, South Dakota, erected by his family and friends.

Photo by Forrest W. Seymour

The mass grave at Wounded Knee and monument, erected by
the Horn Clouds and others, bearing the names of Indian dead.

The worst of the Bad Lands, near the Stronghold Table.

"All right, all right! I'll come with you."

Sitting Bull sent the moaning woman to the other cabin for some clothing, and asked his 17-year-old son, Crow Foot, who had been awakened by the commotion, to saddle up his favorite pony.

"No!" interrupted Bull Head firmly. "You stay right here! I'll have one of my men saddle the horse and bring it around." And he gave the order to one of his policemen just outside the door.

The wife's crying attracted nearby residents, and word raced through the village that the police were there. In a matter of minutes, there was an excited mob milling around outside and encircling the policemen.

As Sitting Bull dressed, he tried to engage Bull Head in debate, but the lieutenant kept urging, "Don't argue, father. There's no use stalling around. Let's not start any trouble. Just get dressed and come along."

At that moment Catch-the-Bear, Sitting Bull's principal bodyguard, came running up to the cabin door, and Bull Head felt his first tremor of fear. There had been bad blood between the two for some years. It had started when a crowd of Standing Rock warriors, led by Sitting Bull, went to visit their Crow and Cheyenne neighbors at the Lame Deer agency in Montana. They were there on issue day, so most of them drew their rations at the Lame Deer commissary. Bull Head and Catch-the-Bear had a small argument over a flour sack in which to carry their groceries, and Bull Head angrily hit his companion in the back. Catch-the-Bear never forgot or forgave the insult, although Sitting Bull tried in various ways to straighten out the quarrel between his bodyguard and the reservation policeman.

The very next day at Lame Deer, the Crows had begun taunting their Sioux visitors about how many times the

Crows had defeated them in battle. In old times, the two tribes had stolen horses from each other for generations because they disliked the chore of breaking young colts to ride. It was much more exciting and manly to steal broken ponies!

The stories the Crows told grew more and more insulting. But Sitting Bull sat, without a word, placidly smoking his pipe and thus demonstrating his self-control. Finally Crazy Head, a Crow warrior, could stand Sitting Bull's superb demeanor no longer. Leaping to his feet, he jerked off his breechcloth, strode across the circle, and waggled his penis back and forth in Sitting Bull's face. The Crows howled with delight, and the Sioux warriors crouched tensely, awaiting a signal from their leader to avenge this intolerable insult.

But Sitting Bull continued calmly to smoke his pipe, staring straight ahead and seeing nothing. Crazy Head returned to his place in the circle and the tension eased. In the end, the Crows gave the Hunkpapa leader and his party thirty fine horses to show their admiration and reassert their friendship. Bull Head, assuming that an agency policeman would be among the first to share in the gift, had just picked a spotted black-and-white for himself when Sitting Bull called out, "Catch-the-Bear, the one Bull Head is holding is yours!"

Humiliated, Bull Head released the pony as his rival jerked the reins away. Then Sitting Bull, having made his point, turned to Bull Head and smiled, "How would you like that little buckskin?" It was a magnificent horse and Bull Head accepted it. But in his heart the bitterness of his abasement before Catch-the-Bear was not assuaged, and now Sitting Bull, too, was drawn close to the web of revenge that Bull Head's mind was spinning.

So the hatred between Catch-the-Bear and Bull Head had smouldered through the years, and at this delicate moment it could no longer be contained. As the policeman emerged from the cabin with a firm hold on Sitting Bull's arm, the crowd outside was angry and ready to take action. All that was needed was a spark, and young Crow Foot provided it.

"Aha!" he mocked his father. "You who have always called yourself a brave chief! And now you allow yourself to be taken by these metal-breasts (police)!"

The taunting by his own son was too much for Sitting Bull. He braced his feet and tried to jerk away from his captors. "All right," he cried out, "why should I go with these tools of the white man? I will not go! I will not!"

Bull Head had been hanging on to one of Sitting Bull's arms, Shave Head the other. They pushed him, struggling, through the mob, Policeman Red Tomahawk closing in behind to prevent attacks on his colleagues. The rest of the police were ahead, trying to force an opening in the milling crowd.

Catch-the-Bear swiftly pressed his way in alongside his old enemy, raised his rifle to his hip, and shot Bull Head in the side point-blank. The wounded man sagged away, but as he did so he drew his revolver and shot the struggling Sitting Bull. At the same instant, Red Tomahawk also fired into the chief's body. That was their order: *Do not let him escape under any circumstances!*

Policeman Alone Man, seeing it all happen, had wheeled and shot Catch-the-Bear, killing him instantly.

The shooting loosed a furious hand-to-hand struggle between the forty policemen and the 100 or more warriors in the crowd. Clubs, knives, guns—every available weapon was in use. As the attackers slipped into the edge of the woods for protection, the policemen dragged their wounded into one of the cabins.

At daybreak, Captain Fechet wisely had started to move

his troops cautiously from the Oak Creek way station toward Sitting Bull's village. They were about three miles from Grand River when the officer saw a rider racing toward them. It was one of Bull Head's police.

"Hurry! Hurry! Trouble, trouble!" he yelled, and Fechet got his cavalrymen into a gallop.

When the troop came over the ridge at Grand River, the police were cooped up in the two cabins and Sitting Bull's corral, with the Hunkpapa warriors firing at them from three sides. The Hotchkiss gun's crew thought the corral was housing the enemy, and it pumped a couple of shells into the area until Alone Man bravely ran out waving a white cloth to stop the firing. The gun then swung toward the woods and it was not long until the warriors' rifles were silenced.

The followers of Sitting Bull now fled in all directions. Many did not even stop to pick up their belongings. Captain Fechet rounded up as many of the Indian women as he could and urged them to go after the fugitives and assure them there would be no more shooting. As soon as he could get the wounded into wagons, he turned his troop back toward Fort Yates in order to calm the Indians' fears. But nothing would stop the flight of many Hunkpapas during the next few days—most of them headed for the Cheyenne River villages of Hump and Big Foot, the nearest refuges they knew.

The sound of guns had not even ended when the wailing of Indian wives and relatives began throughout the community. Four Indian policemen had been killed outright— Little Eagle, Hawk Man, Afraid-of-Soldier, and John Strong Arm. Bull Head and Shave Head both died of their wounds the following day in the hospital at Fort Yates.

Of the Hunkpapa warriors, at least eight were dead including Sitting Bull and his son Crow Foot, Catch-the-

Bear, Black Bird, and Little Assiniboine. A number were known to have been wounded but have fled. Spotted Horn Bull, Brave Thunder and Chase Wounded were severely injured and all three died later. One warrior showed up at Big Foot's camp in a couple of days with a bullet still in his leg.

The relatives of some of the policemen now joined in the death chants. John Strong Arm's family came to the scene to learn what was happening and saw his lifeless body there. One of his relatives, Holy Medicine, seized a neck-yoke lying nearby and smashed the face of Sitting Bull's corpse with a frightful blow.

"What the hell are you doing?" yelled one of Fechet's soldiers. "The man is dead! Leave him alone!"

The undertaker at Fort Yates sealed the frozen body in a box the next day with the smashed jaw still under the left ear. He was ordered to pour quicklime into the rude coffin, and it was put in a grave at one side of the fort burial ground without any ceremony.

Tatanka Iyotanke, the great Sitting Bull, was not only dead, he was physically exterminated.

Realizing that the several hundred Hunkpapas fleeing southward could only cause increasing problems, Agent McLaughlin put couriers on their trail as quickly as possible. These messengers overtook 250 or more along the Moreau River within the next few days and persuaded most of them to return to their homes. Another 150 or so, however, were already beyond reach or would not trust the promises of McLaughlin's scouts. The terror of those Hotchkiss shells had simply been too traumatic.

At Standing Rock, the ghost dance rebellion was over. The Grand River Hunkpapas were without leadership. Those who fled would be wandering ragged and hungry toward the southwest during the next two weeks, hoping to reach Red Cloud's agency and safety, meanwhile watching every ridge furtively for any sign of white soldiers.

But not for long were the Hunkpapas alone in their flight.

On the morning after Big Foot's people got back to their village on Deep Creek, following the ghost dance rendezvous with Hump, the sun was hardly an hour high when the chief had his wagon hitched up and was driving off toward the soldier camp at the fork where the Belle Fourche River flows into the Cheyenne. A number of his headmen accompanied him, some of them taking their wives as Big Foot did. The women put tepee poles and buckskins and hay into their wagons so they could stay a few nights if necessary.

The group was greeted at the camp entrance by Colonel Sumner's aides and his interpreter, Felix Benoit. Big Foot found Bear Eagle and several other minor chiefs from the vicinity already there, paying their respects to the new commanding officer. Some of them were camped among the cottonwoods at the edge of the soldiers' camp, and while Big Foot and his men went forward to present themselves, their wives erected tepees a hundred yards away.

Because Big Foot was chief of them all, the Indians naturally deferred to him. Sumner shook hands with him and then with the others as Benoit introduced them. They made small talk for a little while, smoked their pipes, and finally enjoyed a meal which the officer had his men prepare.

During the next two days the colonel summoned the Indian leaders several times for brief visits. He wanted to get to know them as well as possible. The cavalry officer not only thought he understood the Indian mind better than most in his profession, but he had an unusually humane and compassionate feeling toward his wards.

When, after two or three sessions, he felt the time was right, he said to Big Foot, "I'm sure you know about the trouble the Great Father is having with some of the people south of here. I hope that I can rely on the Minneconjous under my jurisdiction here to follow my advice and remain in their villages."

Big Foot wished to be completely frank. "We are anxious to do whatever is right," he replied through the interpreter. "We have no intention of leaving our homes here, where we are comfortable. But I have to tell you something honestly: We do not get nearly enough rations from the agency to keep us in good health. The young mothers are poorly fed and as a result they have no milk in their breasts for their babies. The children too often get sick and die. If our young warriors are nervous and angry, it is because their families are hungry and they do not get enough clothing to keep them warm through the hard winter."

Big Foot paused a moment while the translation was finished, and then resumed.

"You can tell your soldier chiefs and the Great Father that we do not want to cause any trouble with them. We want only peace. But we cannot have peace unless the Indians get fair treatment. And the agent seems to have no ears for our hunger and nakedness. Still, we wish to be friends and live peaceably."

To Sumner this straightforward statement seemed wholly convincing. From the very beginning he had been well impressed by the big Minneconjou.

Big Foot and his party soon struck their tepees and went along home. But being only a two- or three-hour ride away, some of them dropped into the military camp every few days, and Sumner's patrols moved through the Indian village now and then, greeting the members of the Indian community they passed with a friendly *"Hau, kola!"*

There was some ghost-dancing going on in the neighborhood, however, led by the medicine man Yellow Bird. Disillusioned now, Big Foot paid little attention to it, and apparently neither did Sumner's scouts. But in spite of his assurances to the army officer that his own intentions were utterly peaceable, the chief was not unaware that some of his hotheaded young men clung to the ghost dance doctrine precisely as Kicking Bear had laid it out for them:

"The white soldiers are our enemies! Dakota warriors must remain alert and ready for the moment of emancipation, whenever it may come!"

So Sumner deluded himself that everything was under complete control, and he reported to General Miles:

"I have held a council with all the principal chiefs in this section of the country, and find that they are peaceably disposed and inclined to obey orders; but from their talk, as well as from reports I have received from officers here and others, I believe they are really hungry and suffering from want of clothing and covering. I advise that 1,000 rations be sent me at once for issue to them, and authority to purchase a certain amount of fresh beef."

It was during this critical week that Chief Big Foot received his final and most urgent call from Red Cloud's agency to come to Pine Ridge and help the Oglalas "make a peace." The message was signed first by Red Cloud, but also by No Water, Big Road, Knife Chief, and several other leaders. Of course they were fully aware that Big Foot's protégé, Kicking Bear, was one of the principal ghost dance holdouts, and among other things they thought Big Foot would have some influence with him.

"My dear friend Chief Big Foot," said the letter. "When you receive this, I want you to come at once. When you get to our reservation, a fire is going to be started and I want you to come and help us put it out and make a peace. If you will come among us and make a peace, we will give you 100 head of horses."

A number of the men in Big Foot's council pressed him to accept this invitation from Red Cloud and strike out for Pine Ridge, but the chief realized the risks. He parried the arguments of his hotheads as best he could and stalled for time—always now the procrastinator. He sensed that he could not suppress his radicals much longer unless he took some affirmative step to postpone the threat, and so he conceived the idea of taking the whole band to the Cheyenne River agency on the Missouri River for the next issuance of their annuities, which would occur on December 22.

"We have to get winter clothing and blankets," he insisted.

When Big Foot sent this word to Colonel Sumner, the officer was delighted. He had no hint of the much-argued plan to head for Pine Ridge, but he now realized, as a result of various reports, that there were some very unruly young men in Big Foot's camp. He decided that the Minneconjou chief was "making an extraordinary effort to keep his followers quiet," and he reported this to his superiors.

"It has been a pleasure to have your friendship," said Sumner to the chief. "I am grateful that you have shown peaceable intentions. We could have had trouble if your men had tried to go among the hostiles at Pine Ridge."

"Oh, no," replied Big Foot, "we have no such intentions."
He understood the colonel to mean the hostiles gathered at
the Stronghold, and to go there was the farthest thing from
his mind. Since the whole matter of Red Cloud's invitation
had been deferred until later, he saw no reason to raise it here.

So on the very morning that Sitting Bull was killed on the
Grand River, Big Foot was getting his band started eastward down the Cheyenne, toward the agency at Fort Bennett. He assured his headmen that when they got home
again toward the end of December, he would then decide
whether to accept the Pine Ridge offer of a hundred ponies
for his peacemaking. This took the pressure off him for a
couple of weeks at least.

The second day following found the band encamped 20
miles downriver, halfway to Cherry Creek and across the
Cheyenne from the trading post run by James Cavanaugh
and his two sons. Big Foot thought everything was running
smoothly. But now fate began to close in on him from
every direction.

First of all, Colonel Sumner had finally received orders
from Fort Meade to arrest the Minneconjou chief and bring
him to the fort for imprisonment as a troublemaker in the
ghost dance rebellion. The supreme command of the Army,
startled by Sitting Bull's death in the custody of Indian
police and unable to lay its hands on Kicking Bear and
Short Bull in the Stronghold, concluded that the seizure of
Big Foot now had the highest priority. He was listed as a
dangerous ghost-dance fanatic.

Sumner was naturally embarrassed. He had let his ward
go off unsupervised, and here was the Army proposing to
throw the man in prison as a desperate criminal.

But although Big Foot knew nothing of his imminent
arrest, he did learn that evening, to his dismay, that a lot
of soldiers had crossed the Missouri River from Fort Sully

and were coming up the Cheyenne directly at him from the east. He tried to think what the meaning of this maneuver might be. Why were these strange troops coming to confront him on the east, when his presumed friend, Colonel Sumner, was only a few miles back to the west and supposedly watching over him?

He could not believe that Sumner was deceiving him in his friendly farewell, intending only to trap the band when a supporting force arrived from the opposite direction. Still, he was distressed and uncertain, and he decided just to sit still for a day and watch developments.

Colonel Sumner was of course innocent of any such bad faith, although he knew that Colonel H. C. Merriam and his 7th Infantry, called up by General Miles to help box in the Sioux, had reached Fort Sully, north of Pierre, on December 7. The Missouri was jammed with ice, and Merriam was unable to get his men and supplies across to Fort Bennett until a week later. He then prepared to move up the Cheyenne at a leisurely pace.

Merriam had been warned not to start a stampede of Indians in the vicinity, so he instructed Captain J. W. Hurst, who had been in command at Fort Bennett, to send someone ahead and reassure the villages that the soldiers were merely engaged in peaceable reconnaissance. For this task Hurst chose Lieutenant Harry Hale, who had led Captain Ewers to Hump's village only three weeks earlier. Hale needed an Indian bodyguard—and who better than Chief Hump himself, now again a trusted scout for the white soldiers!

Hump was called in from his newly established camp near the fort and he selected one of his policemen, White Thunder, to accompany him. Hurst also sent along an interpreter named Nolland. This quartet went up the river on December 18 and reached Cheyenne City, the white settlement at the mouth of Cherry Creek, the same night. The only person in sight there was Henry Angell, one of the homesteaders.

"Where are the others?" asked Hale.

"Haven't you heard? Some wild Hunkpapas are coming down Cherry Creek, we're told, and are on the warpath. Our people have all gone off to hide."

Hale thought a few minutes. Then he said to White Thunder, "You go on west and find Colonel Sumner. Tell him what the situation is here. If any of Sitting Bull's people show up, I'll try to handle them until you bring help."

Then Hale spent all the next day visiting with the scattering of Minneconjous who were still living around Hump's former village. They knew Big Foot's band was encamped a few miles west of them, but they didn't seem to know anything about an invasion of Hunkpapas.

At noon on the twentieth, Hump came riding in fast to alert Hale that a sizeable group of horsemen was approaching. The lieutenant went out with him at once and they ran into 45 Hunkpapa warriors who fortunately showed no signs of hostility.

Nolland was a poor interpreter and communication was slow, but finally Hale got it across to them that if they would camp there and remain quiet for a full day, he would come back with an important officer to negotiate with them and would bring no other soldiers.

The tired and hungry Hunkpapas agreed, and they sent some of the warriors back to bring up their straggling camp of women and children.

Hale's great concern was that Big Foot's men would get to these Hunkpapas before he could get orders about what to do with them. He warned Hump to keep a close watch on the fugitives, therefore, and ordered Angell to slaughter a beef and keep them well fed while he was gone. Then the young lieutenant mounted his horse and rode recklessly back to Fort Bennett, covering the 52 miles in less than seven hours. He persuaded Captain Hurst to return with him at once to Cheyenne City. They were accompanied only by a sergeant and two interpreters, and they reached their destination the following afternoon, December 21.

The arrival of Hump and Lieutenant Hale at Cherry Creek had of course been reported to Chief Big Foot by his scouts. Puzzled about what was going on here, the chief was doubly grateful that he had delayed his trip eastward.

Things began to be clarified the next day when two Hunkpapas strode into his camp, one with a bullet in his leg, and asked for Big Foot. In the quiet of his lodge, they told him the story of the fight with the agent's Indian police at Grand River and the killing of Sitting Bull.

Big Foot was badly shaken by the news. An indistinct presentiment whispered to him that he would somehow be caught in this fateful web of events. He emerged from his lodge weeping, not from any sense of fear but only maddening perplexity.

"I do not understand how they dared kill our Hunkpapa brother!" he kept repeating.

But shortly he said to himself that they must not allow

this outrage to turn them toward any foolish acts. He must get his people busy, he thought. So he summoned his council and announced, "There is no more grass on this side of the river, so we will move across to the other side."

Everyone promptly got to work moving. The Cavanaughs had been worried enough, what with the Minneconjous across the river and reports of warlike Hunkpapas coming down the Cherry Creek. Now that Big Foot's people had moved across to the front yard of their store, they were in a mild panic. Without stopping to bolt their doors, they fled westward in the direction of Colonel Sumner to find protection.

Chief Big Foot realized that there would probably be a lot of Hunkpapas in flight as a result of Sitting Bull's death, and the next morning he sent out a band of ten warriors, one of whom was Dewey Horn Cloud, to move along Cherry Creek and offer the hospitality of his camp to any fugitives who might be found.

In mid-afternoon these emissaries came upon a small group of Hunkpapa women and children with very little clothing, hungry and cold around their campfire, moaning and singing death chants for those slain at Grand River. Their menfolk, they said, were across the Cheyenne River in council with a white soldier.

Big Foot's men immediately went across the river, where they found not only the Hunkpapa warriors, but also Hump and some of the local Minneconjous. Hump and his companions were of course urging the Sitting Bull fugitives to surrender when Lieutenant Hale returned from his race to Fort Bennett.

"Now what do you intruders want?" demanded Hump of the Big Foot party.

Dewey Horn Cloud, whose father was a first cousin of Hump's, stepped forward. "Chief Big Foot sent us only to offer Sitting Bull's people food and lodging. We will feed and clothe them, and then you can do with them as you wish."

Hump, now again the confirmed Army scout, thought there was more to it than that.

"Do you think I am without brains?" he shouted. "They don't need to go to Big Foot's camp. I am going to take them all to the agency as soon as Lieutenant Hale gets back. I know your intentions! You people want a fight! I am going to bring some infantry that will give you plenty of fight, since that's what you want!"

The former Hump warriors from around Cherry Creek arose and surrounded Big Foot's men, but the Hunkpapas leaped between the two Minneconjou groups and said to Hump, "Look, father, do not start a fight or we will have to side with our friends from Big Foot's people. Have they not offered to feed us and help us?"

Hump grew quiet. Shortly he called out, "Who will stay with me and hear what the officers have to say when they return?"

About 60 warriors, Hunkpapas and Minneconjous, moved over to Hump's side of the circle. With their women and children they represented about 200 Indians.

A few of Hump's former followers and 14 of the Hunkpapa refugees, unwilling to risk entrapment by the white soldiers, elected to follow Big Foot's men and join his trek, wherever it might lead them. They withdrew at once, gathered up their families, and moved west to Big Foot's camp.

Finding Cavanaugh's store unlocked and unattended, some of the Hunkpapas went in and helped themselves. When Big Foot learned of this he was furious, and had the whole camp searched to make certain his own people had not stolen any of Cavanaugh's goods.

Hurst and Hale reached Cheyenne City the next day,

and they had two beeves slaughtered to provide a grand feast for those who had stayed with Hump. Then Captain Hurst made a speech to them:

"My good friends, I am not here to deceive you. I speak with a straight tongue, and you can take my offer or leave it. I want you to give up your guns and go to Fort Bennett with me. There you will be well fed and clothed. I do not make any promises for the future which I cannot fulfill. I can only tell you that you will not gain anything by joining Big Foot. The Army is going to demand that he, also, obey the orders that have been given him. If you go to him and he disobeys the Army, you will probably be destroyed—and your families also."

The Hunkpapa warriors talked until the middle of the night. Then they walked out and laid down their guns in front of Captain Hurst and Lieutenant Hale. Eight hours later the camp was packed up and moving eastward toward the agency, 166 Hunkpapas in all, and 55 remaining Cherry Creek Minneconjous.

The next day this caravan passed Colonel Merriam's infantry, headed west on the Cheyenne River road. Big Foot had been informed that these bluecoats were getting near, and he was worried.

"I don't see how we can continue eastward to the agency with these strange soldiers in our path, and with Hump threatening to have them attack us," he said to his headmen. "I think we should just return to our village for the present."

But before he could act, Colonel Sumner resolved the dilemma for him.

Late on December 19 one of Sumner's patrols came in with both White Thunder, Hump's scout, and the three Cavanaughs. They reported that Big Foot was still at Cherry Creek and apparently expecting to meet a crowd of Sitting Bull's fugitives there.

Sumner saw that he was going to be in serious trouble shortly if this kind of conjunction occurred, and the next morning he mounted most of his cavalry and started eastward. The outfit camped that night at Narcisse Narcelle's ranch, and then started moving again toward Cherry Creek.

Big Foot's scouts discovered this movement and the chief realized he was being hemmed in. But after all, he knew Colonel Sumner well, and he had no idea what threat to his band's safety might be represented by the troops coming from the east. So he called a council quickly and told his headmen that he was going to straighten things out with Sumner at once.

"I do not want any warriors with me," he said, "in case we have displeased him. I do not want to give the soldiers any pretext for shooting at us."

Shedding Bear stepped forward and said quietly, "Father, we cannot let you go alone. I will go with you to see that no harm comes to you."

"All right," the chief replied, "and I also want the two runners from Standing Rock to come with us so that I can explain to the soldier chief why we have been waiting here to help Sitting Bull's people in their distress."

Big Foot was hoarse and coughing frequently. He had the grippe and was feeling miserable. The headmen helped him into a light wagon which Shedding Bear drove, and the two Hunkpapas rode ponies. They were only a few miles down the road toward Narcelle's ranch when they saw Sumner's whole command coming, so they pulled up and waited. In a few minutes, Sumner himself had ridden up to the wagon.

The officer realized that he needed to take a tough stance with the Minneconjous now. He had foolishly allowed them to slip out of his hands once, and it mustn't happen again. Moreover, he had assured his superiors that the band was on its way to Fort Bennett and that its chief could be arrested there, whereas it was plain that the Indians had not done what they said they were going to do.

"*Sitanka,*" said the colonel through Felix Benoit, his interpreter, "I am surprised at you. I thought we were friends and I could trust your word." He had spoken Big Foot's name in Siouan deliberately to reassure him.

"There is no reason for you to doubt my word," said Big Foot. "I am ready to follow any orders you wish to give me, and all my men will do the same."

He fell into a fit of coughing and Sumner could see plainly that he was not well.

After wiping his mouth and forehead, the chief looked up as Sumner continued. "Well, what do you mean by harboring these Hunkpapas here? You know that they are Sitting Bull's men and that they belong up at Standing Rock. They have no business here!"

Big Foot looked sad and smiled. "My father," he said

softly, "what does the white man do if all of a sudden he comes upon some of his brothers and other relatives who are sick and cold and hungry, who had to run away without clothing or blankets? Does he say to them, 'I am sorry, you are in the wrong place?' No, I do not believe this. I think he will feed them and give them coats and blankets and let them rest a little while."

When this was translated by Benoit, Sumner could see that he would never win that argument, and he remained quiet as Big Foot continued.

"Not only these two brothers, who brought us the sad word of Sitting Bull's death, but a great many of our kinsmen, the Hunkpapas, are near here at Cherry Creek. We offered them the hospitality of our camp, and I did not dare to go on to the agency for our supplies until they were cared for. Their shoes and moccasins were all worn out and they had nothing to wear on their feet, because they ran away from the guns of the soldiers on Grand River. Do you say this was wrong of Big Foot and his people?"

Sumner could not avoid looking at the two Hunkpapas, one of whom had had the bullet pried out of his leg the day before. They were a sorry pair indeed—ragged and plainly trail-worn.

The colonel smiled wryly. "All right, we can talk about that later. But I am not permitted to let you go on to Fort Bennett now. We have all got to go back west."

He allowed it to sound as if they were going home to Big Foot's village on Deep Creek, but he knew that he was going to have to take them right past the village to his own military camp, and then keep herding them along to Fort Meade. And above all, he did not dare tell the Indian chief that he was soon to be arrested.

Big Foot, on his part, was somewhat relieved because

Sumner was not pressing him eastward into the vise of Merriam's troops.

"Yes, we wish to go back there with you," he said pleasantly. "I will send down to Cherry Creek for our rations later. Anyway, some soldiers are coming up the Cheyenne and they will take care of the Hunkpapa refugees who have not joined my camp."

"What's that?" said Sumner, startled. He turned sharply to Benoit. "What's he saying? How many of the Hunkpapas do they have among them here?"

Benoit repeated the question and Big Foot said, "Only 35 or 40. They want to live with us."

Sumner thought for a moment and then said with resignation, "Well, there's nothing for it now but to let them come along." He knew that he would never be able to sort out the strangers anyway. And he sensed that he had better get Big Foot's band away from the other Hunkpapas as quickly as possible. Merriam would be rounding up the rest, unless they went on to Fort Bennett voluntarily.

He turned to Captain Henissee. "Captain, take a few men and go back to the chief's camp with him. Round up every last one of his outfit and get them started in this direction. We'll start moving back to Narcelle's."

So in two hours the whole Minneconjou encampment was trailing down the river road westward, and they camped that night near the troops at the Narcelle ranch. Sumner stationed guards on all sides, lest the Indians' behavior take some new unexpected turn. He had had the caravan counted as it came down the road. His aides made it 333 Indians, including the 38 Hunkpapas. Big Foot's Minneconjous had been augmented some by the remnants of Hump's old village and by a handful of Oglala wanderers headed homeward to Pine Ridge, who had joined up just for the companionship.

Sumner's troop had ample supplies, and he ordered eight beeves loosed from the livestock so the warriors could ride them down and shoot them for butchering. It was probably the Indian in Benoit that rebelled at this device. He quickly moved among some of Big Foot's headmen and spoke quietly.

"The soldier chief will know how many guns you have if you all ride out to shoot the cattle. Perhaps he intends to gather them up later."

The word was passed along, and as the cattle were turned out no one moved. Benoit himself rode forward and calmly shot the animals, one after another.

In council that evening, Big Foot was disturbed about all this.

"Now why would he want to take away our guns? We do not wish to do any harm. We do not want war. We do not want any fighting. I have told him that. I do not understand."

He would have understood better if he had known of the order for his arrest which Sumner bore in his pocket.

Ironically, Big Foot never learned of it. And partly for that reason he made a fatal misjudgment about the matter of guns a few days later.

CHAPTER IV

THE FLIGHT

The next morning before sunrise Benoit was trotting around through the Indian camp giving instructions. Big Foot's people had about forty wagons altogether, and of course innumerable travois and loaded ponies carrying extra tepee poles and supplies.

Colonel Sumner wanted the company to move along sharply, so he ordered the women and children and old men to get into the wagons. Big Foot's wagon was brought up to the head of the column, and the train as a whole was divided into three sections, each guarded by a troop of soldiers. The warriors on their ponies were held back to accompany the third section, followed by a troop of infantry.

Big Foot's men didn't like this arrangement from the beginning, but they made no open protest until two wagons in the second section tried to pass out of Narcelle's gate at the same time and got their wheels locked together. The horses pulling the jammed wagons reared and kicked, getting their legs over the traces, and shortly the two rigs were thoroughly tangled. The women who were driving were frightened and screaming, children began to wail, and heavy clouds of dust rolled up around the stomping horses.

The cavalrymen, somewhat on edge anyway, rode around yelling hoarsely at the Indian women drivers.

"All right, you squaws, get that god-damned thing out of there. Back 'em up! Pull 'em over this way! Hey, you! Get down there and untangle that harness. . . ."

Black Fox, son-in-law of Big Foot, listened to this for a few seconds and then, throwing off his coat, grabbed his gun from a wagon nearby. "I don't care to have my relatives abused this way by any white man!" he shouted, raising his rifle toward the officer.

Benoit, who understood the Siouan words as well as the tone, yelled at the officer, "Look out! Get the hell out of there!"

Fortunately the cavalryman looked up, saw Black Fox coming, and spurred his horse out of the vicinity. Other warriors promptly rallied around Black Fox.

"Are we going to take any more of this insolence?" they asked each other. "Let's go up ahead and join our families, where we belong!"

The tangled wagons were disengaged at last, the gate was cleared, and a couple of dozen warriors raced out on their ponies, shrieking war cries and waving their rifles as they came forward. A bugler up ahead blew an alarm.

The women driving the wagons in the first two sections looked back and saw the Indian men coming at full speed. Thinking that some kind of break was about to occur, they began heaving pots and kettles and tepee poles and other gear from their wagons so they could run for their lives with less impedimenta. This racket was mixed with the screaming and wailing of both women and children. The whole scene was one of pandemonium.

The cavalry troop at the head of the column was ordered quickly into a skirmish line with rifles ready, and the Indian attack suddenly collapsed before this show of strength. After milling around for a minute or two, the warriors wandered back toward the second and third sections of the train.

Colonel Sumner galloped up to Big Foot's wagon, which the chief himself was driving.

"What the hell is going on back there?" he demanded. His interpreter was still far to the rear, but Big Foot comprehended readily enough, and he laughed as if it was a matter of little importance. Summoning up his best English, he said haltingly, "Old womans . . . holler."

Sumner didn't see any humor in it. "Well, my friend, we can't have this sort of thing! You have it stopped!" And he pointed to the chief's pony, which was tied to the tailgate of the wagon.

Big Foot understood. He immediately mounted his horse and rode about asking the people to quiet down and keep good order. He also sent some of his headmen to the rear to tell the warriors to do as the soldiers asked them. But the young men were angry, and the women remained apprehensive about what was going to happen to them.

Still Sumner saw nothing to be greatly concerned about. When Big Foot returned to his wagon, the colonel called Benoit over and said, "Tell the chief that since we have all these Hunkpapas mixed in here, I want everyone to go straight to my camp and stay there until we can sort them out."

The explanation was made and Chief Big Foot nodded his head in acquiesence, seemingly undisturbed. But he knew very well that it was not going to be as simple as the white soldier chief imagined.

It was late afternoon when the head of the long column neared the cluster of log cabins which was Big Foot's village. The cavalrymen on the flanks had been told to keep the train straight on the road to the military camp, eight miles farther up the river. But sounds of trouble began to arise. The women in the wagons were calling to each other in excited tones, and some wailing began. The warriors were dashing wildly around again, a few racing their mounts once more to the van of the cavalcade to show their displeasure.

Now Colonel Sumner began to sense that his problem

was no small one. He realized that any real confrontation with these irritable Indian men might easily mean shooting, and that would be the end of any successful mission. It was all very well for his superiors, including General Miles, to dash off orders blithely about keeping a firm hand and not letting the quarry escape under any circumstances. But even ignoring the warriors, here were 200 women and children, a lot of whom were going to be maimed or killed if a fracas was permitted to start.

In the midst of this mild panic in Sumner's breast, Chief Big Foot's wagon came rumbling up behind him and the officer turned to see what was going on. The chief, whose cough had become somewhat worse, had been lying down under some blankets in the wagon while his wife drove, but now he was sitting up to speak. When he finished, Benoit translated:

"The chief says he will go with you to your camp, but these women are all cold and hungry and they want to go to their own homes here. There's going to be trouble, he thinks, if they're told they cannot go home."

As Benoit finished, Big Foot began to speak again, this time with some emotion.

"He says this is their home where the government told them to stay," Benoit continued. "He says that none of these people have done anything that justifies their removal by force; so take me, Big Foot, to your camp if you must, and leave these people here."

Sumner's mind was in a turmoil. After all, it was going to be dark soon and there was no disputing that the people were cold and tired. The emotional pull of their own homes was irresistible, of course. What could be lost by letting them quiet down overnight? He could proceed with the plan in the morning.

He summoned Lieutenant Duff, his aide, who was sitting on his mount at one side.

"I'm afraid we'll bring on a fight if we don't let these people turn in here, Duff. It appears that we'd have to use force to prevent it, and in that case we'll be charged with the attack and probably held responsible for the killing of peaceable Indians at their own village. I don't like the smell of that."

Sumner was also thinking of the probable loss of men in his own command, but he didn't mention it.

Duff nodded and sat silent.

"Tell the people they can go on in," called the colonel to Benoit, "but I want the chief to stay right here for the moment."

During this discussion the column was in fact already breaking up. The soldiers could not have stopped it without using their arms, and they had received no such order.

When the word passed along that everyone could go to his own home, there was a great yelling and rattling of wagons, and the remainder of the caravan dispersed in a matter of minutes.

Sumner was still trying to decide what to do about Chief Big Foot. Obviously his charge was to keep the man under arrest. But it was not Big Foot who was causing him concern; it was the hot-blooded young warriors. If he hauled the chief off to the "camp of observation," it was more than likely that the fighting men, lacking the chief's restraining influence, would organize during the night in an effort to free him or possibly even make a break for the Bad Lands. And that, in either case, would mean endless tragedy all around.

"My friend," he finally said to Big Foot, "can I have your word that you will come to Camp Cheyenne for a council in the morning and bring with you all of the

Standing Rock Hunkpapas? I am ordered to take them into my protection, and they must come with you. The rest of the people can stay here in the village until I give them further orders."

The chief was grateful for this solution, and he gave his assurance readily. His wagon lumbered away into the trees. A few loud orders rang through the crisp air, and the column of horsemen and supply wagons and infantry moved off westward, arriving at its base camp shortly after sunset.

It was December 22. Late that night a courier rode into Camp Cheyenne from Fort Meade, bearing a telegram from General Miles. The Army chieftain had come himself to Rapid City in the Black Hills five days earlier to take personal charge of this wide-scale campaign against the Sioux Indians.

The wire for Colonel Sumner said, among other things:

"You had better push on rapidly to Meade with your prisoners, be careful they do not escape, and look out for other Indians."

Sumner did not really have any "prisoners," of course. The "other Indians" to whom Miles referred were, first of all, the remnants of the ghost dance rebels who were still loitering in the region of the Stronghold under Kicking Bear and Short Bull; but even more importantly, a reported band of stragglers from the Sitting Bull fight headed south from the western edge of North Dakota.

Colonel Sumner was supposed to be guarding the settlements northeast of the Black Hills, as well as the Cheyenne Forks area, and the threat of "other Indians"— which turned out to be totally false—threw his logic off the track at a critical moment. He first sent a reply to General Miles saying that if Big Foot did not come in as promised the next morning, he would send his cavalry down to the village and take him by whatever means were necessary.

Yet in fact Sumner stalled around all the next forenoon waiting for Big Foot to show up, or for his Army scouts to return and report what was wrong. It is true that the imaginary Indians from North Dakota were on his mind, and he hesitated to take his command eastward from the camp if there was serious danger from the other quarter. Moreover, to seize Big Foot probably meant a major skirmish, with losses on both sides. Many of the Minneconjous were now in log cabins, which gave them a strong defense.

The officer saw no neat solution for this dilemma. He wished desperately that he could unload it. Suddenly this thought occured to him:

Suppose he could get Big Foot now at last to agree to go straight to the band's agency at Fort Bennett on the Missouri, this time without loitering. The chief could be arrested there if the Army wished, and Merriam was somewhere in between to keep an eye on things. This would take the troublesome Minneconjous off his hands, leaving him free to turn his attention toward the northwest and intercept the reported Indian renegades there, meanwhile herding the errant Hunkpapas to Fort Meade. After all, he said to himself, he had received no *direct* order to take Big Foot's people by force.

The colonel called his aides together and explained his decision.

"Big Foot's men will either go to the agency or invite a fight. If the latter, then they have made the choice, not I."

By noon, nothing had been heard from Big Foot and Sumner realized that he dared temporize no longer. He gave orders for getting his troops on the march. He was hastily finishing his lunch when a neighboring rancher named John Dunn came through the Army camp, as he frequently did, with a supply of eggs and butter for sale. Sumner knew that Dunn and Big Foot had been acquainted for a good many years, and an idea struck him.

"John, come in here!" he called. "I'm glad to see you. I need your help. How can we persuade Big Foot's people to go to the mouth of the Cheyenne and surrender themselves to the agency authorities? If they refuse to do this, I've got to go in there—fight or no fight—take their guns away from them, and march them to Meade."

Dunn saw clearly the implications of all this and he didn't like the sound of it at all. He made a number of excuses. He had left his wife alone at the ranch, some ten miles distant, and needed to hurry back there. The Minneconjous wouldn't listen to him on such a matter anyway. And he had a ranch and livestock at stake, so he didn't relish the idea of angering Big Foot's wild ones.

Colonel Sumner, feeling somewhat desperate now, would not take no for an answer. He kept at it, and finally Dunn agreed to go down and do the best he could. Felix Benoit went along to find out what had happened to the Indian scouts who had failed to report.

As the two men rode into the Indian village, they met the scouts, Charging First and His Horse Looking, who were at last starting their return to Sumner's camp.

"Where the devil have you fellows been all day?" demanded Benoit, and he stood talking to them as Dunn rode on into the Indian camp. The scouts explained that the Standing Rock Hunkpapas had skipped out during the night, apparently forewarned of Sumner's intention to arrest them. Chief Big Foot was embarrassed, the scouts said, because he had promised the colonel to bring the Hunkpapas with him into Camp Cheyenne, and he had had his scouts out all morning trying to find the fugitives and bring them back.

"We have been waiting to see if they returned," said Charging First.

It was a plausible story.

Meanwhile, Dunn, whom the Indians called Red Beard, had reached Big Foot's cabin. The chief's wife met him at the door, shook hands, and invited him in. Big Foot was lying on the bed, but he arose. Several other Indians, sensing that Dunn brought news of some sort, entered the cabin.

"*Sitanka*," said the rancher, "I just came from the soldiers' camp. The commanding officer asked me to see you. He wants to know why you have not come up there today as you promised. He said he had thought you were a man of your word. He had treated you as one to be trusted."

Big Foot sat down on the edge of the bed. "I am sick," he said. "I have been feeling very bad all day."

Dunn could see that this was true.

"Well, since you didn't come in as you said you would, he now wants you to take your people and go down to Fort Bennett. . . ."

The chief looked up sharply. There was a distinct trace of anger in his face, and Dunn hesitated.

"If he wants us to go to Bennett," said Big Foot, "why did he not send us there when he met us at Cherry Creek, two days ago? Why has he hauled us all the way back here, only to tell us now to start out again immediately on that long march eastward? I do not understand such nonsense!"

Big Foot was now persuaded that the approach of Merriam's troops from Fort Bennett had something to do with all of this stalling and changing of orders.

"My friend," said Dunn, "I was not at Cherry Creek and I do not know why he brought you back. But I am sure that he is bringing his soldiers now to force you to do as he says. You and I have known each other a long time,

Sitanka, and I beg you, as a friend, to do what the soldier chief asks. I would not like to see a single white man killed nor a single Indian either. The white soldiers do not want to kill any warriors unless they are compelled to. If you wish to keep your guns and save your lives, then you had better do what the officer tells you."

The rancher spoke the Siouan tongue fluently, and he had put the case persuasively. All was quiet for a moment, then he continued, "Now it's sundown and I've got twenty miles to go. Do you want me to tell the colonel anything when I pass his camp?"

Big Foot had a short coughing fit and then looked up. "All right, tell him we will go to Bennett in the morning. We do not want a fight."

"I am glad to hear you say so," said Dunn gently. "For once it starts, there is no telling where it will stop. Now tell me, do you still have the Standing Rock Hunkpapas? The colonel wants to know."

The chief was not prepared to discuss this embarrassing subject yet with anyone but his headmen, and he answered "Yes." He had been sleeping and he hoped the fugitives had been rounded up, because among other things they had taken five ponies from the Minneconjou herd. The truth was, however, that Big Foot's men had taken pity on the Hunkpapas because of their fear of arrest, and had let them go—ponies and all.

At this point Felix Benoit and the two scouts came in the door of Big Foot's cabin. Dunn turned to shake hands with the chief and said, "*Sitanka*, my wife is alone at the ranch, and I've got to hurry back. Felix, ask these people what I have told them, and tell them that it's true." He wanted to get away from this mare's nest.

A number of warriors had come crowding into the cabin, one or two at a time. Chief Big Foot now called out to the crowd as Dunn threaded his way out:

"I am ordered that we must all go to Bennett in the morning. If we don't, Red Beard tells me, the soldiers will come and make us go. They will shoot us if they have to!" There was bitterness in his voice.

Dunn did not turn, but went out the door and started home.

"Felix," said Big Foot, "is it true that the colonel sent Red Beard here to tell us this?"

"Yes," replied Benoit, "the colonel sent him to tell you that he wants you to go to Fort Bennett."

The chief looked weary.

"So we will go in the morning, then," he said hoarsely.

The interpreter and his scouts turned and walked back to where their horses were tied. In another minute they were gone.

Big Foot's mind was in a whirl.

"My brothers," he said finally to the men around him, "I am much troubled by what is going on here—" He was stopped by his coughing. When he recovered his voice, he went on:

"First I was headed for Fort Bennett to get our rations and they came and got us and brought us back here merely because we were trying to help our Hunkpapa relatives. Now I am told that I must start again for Bennett tomorrow morning or the soldiers will come in and shoot us and arrest us. We know and they know that there are many soldiers coming toward us on the Cheyenne, and now we are to be driven straight into their midst. What is the meaning of all this?"

A general commotion of debate began among the headmen. Some wanted to start for the agency at once, feeling their way around Merriam's troops. Several wanted to head for Pine Ridge, in acceptance of the peacemaking offer from Red Cloud and his associates.

Big Foot managed to wave off both of these proposals in favor of temporizing again.

"Let us break camp and move up into the hills to the south," he proposed, "until we find out exactly what the white soldier chief intends. If everything is quiet we can come back down here in the morning, or we can start east to Bennett. Meanwhile our women and children will be out in the open and able to get away from the shooting if there is any trouble."

He stopped and coughed violently for a little while, and his voice was hoarse and subdued when he spoke again.

"This is my home. This is my place. If they want to come here and kill me, let them come. I have done no wrong to the white people."

The families turned quickly to the business of rounding up ponies, lashing loads on their backs, and filling wagons.

"My heart is bitter about the threat to shoot us," Big Foot mumbled. "What have we done except obey the soldier chief?"

Riding away from the village toward the setting sun, Benoit and the two scouts looked back to notice wagons being loaded with hay and tepee poles, around the fringe of the grove.

"Now what do you s'pose that means?" Benoit mused.

"They must intend to start for Fort Bennett at once."

He stood looking for a minute or two and then said, "Charging First, you go back down the gully there and watch them until it gets dark. Then come back to camp and report."

Five miles down the road, Benoit and His Horse Looking ran into Colonel Sumner and the cavalry, bivouacked for the night. The officer had decided to move up close enough to act quickly the next morning.

But if Charging First was watching the Indians, there was also someone watching the soldiers. Big Foot had sent Dewey Horn Cloud and a couple of companions to check on the troops, and now that the cavalry had moved back toward Deep Creek and bivouacked, the Minneconjou warriors were galloping back to report.

"He surely means to attack us in the morning," they told their chief, "or else to drive us headlong into the soldiers coming from Cherry Creek."

A half hour later Charging First returned to Sumner's camp. As dark fell, he said, Big Foot's women and children were moaning and crying as they do when they sense a fight coming. But they were all busy packing, as if for immediate departure. And they were loading only a few wagons. Instead, they were packing tepee poles and canvas on ponies, which meant that they intended to move fast and over rough country if necessary.

Sumner called up Iron Shield, another scout. "Race down there and tell them they must not leave until morning! And tell the chief that I want him, personally, down here to talk with me before they leave, as he was supposed to do earlier today!" Iron Shield and Charging First rode off.

Among other things, the colonel wanted those Hunkpapa fugitives, or else a good explanation of where they had gone.

But Iron Shield was too late. He returned to Sumner in the middle of the evening to report that the Minneconjous were moving into the hills along Deep Creek. Maybe they were going to Fort Bennett by the ridge road so as to avoid Colonel Merriam's troops, or maybe they were heading for Pine Ridge—he couldn't tell.

Sumner saw that he was in trouble again. If everything were normal, the Indians would not be starting the long trip to the agency at night—especially after having just completed a difficult trip back to their home village.

He got his troop mounted at once and started toward Big Foot's village. As a precaution, he sent off a message by courier to Colonel Eugene A. Carr, whose 6th Cavalry was sweeping the Bad Lands to the south, warning him that Big Foot might be headed in that direction.

Neither Sumner nor his scouts realized what a panic Big Foot's people were experiencing, and therefore they totally misjudged the speed with which the Minneconjous would move. The whole band, with its livestock and all, was eight miles up Deep Creek and pulling eastward onto high ground by the time Sumner learned they had got away. Finally they were compelled to stop for breath and Big Foot, sick in his wagon, called his council together in the darkness to find out what was happening.

The headmen now issued an ultimatum to their chief: They had been threshing the thing over as they moved, and at last there was an overwhelming majority in favor of striking out for Pine Ridge. They did not like being pinched between Sumner and Merriam any longer, and they had become very suspicious of Sumner's devious maneuvers during the last few days anyway—especially after he began to move against their village in the night!

Now they were out on the open prairie, with nothing between them and Red Cloud's people, so why not just keep going and leave the white soldiers' trap behind?

Big Foot was depressed. He had promised Sumner that they would not try to run away, that they wanted only peace. Now he was put in the position of deliberately deceiving the white officer. Moreover, he was seriously ill and he did not look forward to the long, hard ride to Pine Ridge agency—almost twice as far as Fort Bennett. Already he was confined to his bed of blankets because of his misery. He could no more than sit up when it was necessary to give orders, and his wife had to help him get to the edge of the wagon each time he needed to relieve himself.

And another thing, he warned his council: "You will be lucky if you get to Pine Ridge ahead of a blizzard, this late into the winter!"

If the Minneconjou chief had been a well man, he probably could have recovered his influence and forced a turn toward Fort Bennett, where they were supposed to go. As it was, his headmen refused to alter their decision.

At midnight the band was at the high point of the ridge and about to drift down toward the north fork of the Bad River. Here it was overtaken by Charging First, who, instead of returning to Colonel Sumner with Iron Shield, had decided to set himself on Big Foot's trail and find out what was going on. He rode directly to Big Foot's wagon near the head of the train, and asked the chief what he was doing.

Big Foot raised himself awkwardly and said, "Tell your soldier chief that I wanted to go to Fort Bennett, but my people would not let me. They are afraid of the soldiers that are coming that way. They want to go to Pine Ridge, so I must take them there."

Charging First got back to Big Foot's deserted village before daybreak, just as Sumner's column was arriving there, and the scout reported what Big Foot had said. The officer was swept by a sense of failure and despair. He

realized that Big Foot's men had outsmarted him by running the band in such a frantic march. They would be
twenty-five miles away this very minute, and far out of
his jurisdiction before he could overtake them. Indeed, they
were already halfway to the Bad Lands region where
Carr's troops were stalking Kicking Bear and Short Bull to
prevent their escape northward from the Stronghold.

Well, he had alerted Carr. And the threat of wild Indians north of the Black Hills still had him worried, so he
turned his troop back to Camp Cheyenne. There, once
more too late, a courier arrived with further news from
General Miles: The report of hostile Indians to the north
had turned out to be totally false!

"The attitude of Big Foot has been defiant and hostile,"
the telegram continued, "and you are authorized to arrest
him or any of his people and to take him to Meade or Bennett. . . . The division commander directs, therefore, that
you secure Big Foot and the Cheyenne River Indians, and the
Standing Rock Indians, and if necessary round up the whole
camp and disarm them, and take them to Meade or Bennett."

There was nothing left for Sumner but to send word to
General Miles and Carr of Big Foot's mortifying escape,
and to hope that his colleague to the south could intercept
the fugitives. The explosion that would occur in General
Miles' headquarters at Rapid City when word came that he
had lost his prisoners again, Sumner could foresee all too
readily.

He was not disappointed. "I cannot understand your
telegram of the 22d," the general wired, "stating that Big
Foot's band of Indians to number of 330 had surrendered.
. . . You have two Hotchkiss guns and over 200 men, which
certainly ought to be enough to handle 100 warriors in any
place. . . . Your orders were positive, and you have missed
your opportunity. . . ."

Sumner slammed his fist against a tent pole.
"These bastards in their swivel chairs—" he muttered.

At dawn on the twenty-fourth of December, the exhausted Minneconjous heard gratefully the order to stop
along the banks of the tiny north fork of the Bad River. The
livestock as well as the human beings needed water badly.

Although there was heavy ice on the creek, fall weather
had prevailed in Dakota far later than usual. Whites and
Indians alike knew that a blizzard could be expected at any
time, as Big Foot had warned. A Dakota blizzard, roaring
down on the prairies from the Canadian Rockies, was a
serious enough matter for a primitive people even when
they were tucked away in their winter homes. But out in
the open, with no shelter from the wind and snow except
their tepees, and with the possibility of temperatures which
sometimes drop to 30 degrees or more below zero, death by
freezing or starvation was by no means unknown.

All of the adult members of the band were thinking of
this threat now because a raw north wind had come up,
and it was plainly growing colder. Those who could pulled
their rigs and ponies in among the scraggly cottonwoods
that lined the creek here and there, but the thin row of
trees was little protection.

As soon as the horses were staked out, the warriors were

breaking the river's ice and dipping pails in. The band had been moving almost at a trot for more than twelve hours. Fires were hurriedly built and bits of food warmed, especially for the children and babies. Many adults dropped on blankets or crawled under their wagons and fell asleep.

Women here and there were moaning softly and singing death chants, as was their wont when they felt over-whelming peril to be near. Dewey Horn Cloud, once more assigned to guard the trail behind them, stopped among one group of women and said, "Look, sisters, some of us are on our way back to see whether the soldiers are follow-ing us. Stop your sorrowing until I return, and if there is reason to sing death chants I will tell you truthfully."

But in about two hours Big Foot's headmen had become nervous about the delay, and the camp was roused for a new push. During the forenoon they crossed two or three small creeks, still moving at the same hurried pace. Dewey Horn Cloud and his companion scouts overtook the train toward midday and reported no sign whatever of soldiers in the rear. This relaxed the tension a good deal.

By driving hard, the leaders got the caravan all the way to Cottonwood Creek by early afternoon, where they stopped again for food and rest. But the pause lasted hardly more than an hour, and they were hustled on again. All afternoon the headmen rode up and down the column reassuring and encouraging the weary people.

Just before sunset, the families at the head of the column pulled up to the edge of a precipice, laced with a series of almost vertical gullies, which is the north wall of the Bad Lands. They looked at the long shadows across the Bad Lands floor below them. The old trail plainly had been eroded away long since by some rare rainstorm whose rushing torrents tore deep gashes in the soft clay walls.

It was a maddening blow, for there was not a single

point visible where the caravan could descend—and there was a half-mile train of horses and wagons loaded with sleeping children and exhausted adults behind them, moving forward to the wall's edge.

The raw wind told everyone that somehow they had to get down there into the protection of the clay buttes below. Big Foot was coughing much of the time now, and had begun to spit up blood. He called the headmen around his wagon and they discussed the problem.

Shortly the warriors rode back among the wagons asking for shovels and spades and axes, and a work crew of five-dozen men began to hack a narrow roadway out of the side of the shallowest gully nearby that led to the bottom.

The sun had gone down when the last of the wagons descended, rattling and sliding down the steep, powdered path. A couple of wagons had tipped over, but without serious injury to anyone, since most of the people had gone down the grade on foot.

Even now, however, there was no respite. The band had to have water. "Keep moving! Keep moving!" insisted the headmen.

As the long column wound among the clay humps and giant footstools, eerie reflections of the evening's light played tricks on their eyes and senses. It was a full two hours more to the White River. Then suddenly before them in the darkness was that beautiful field of white ice, with water beneath.

"Get across! Get across!" the headmen called. They wanted that precarious barrier between them and whatever lay behind.

In slightly more than 24 hours, Big Foot's band of 300 Minneconjous had marched approximately sixty miles with very limited supplies of food, little bedding or extra clothing, using no shelter and getting only snatches of rest. It is little wonder that the troops who were looking for Big

Foot were confused. Almost every strategist among the military was preoccupied with the assumption that the Minneconjous were trying to join up with the Stronghold rebels.

This idea was no doubt in the backs of the minds of a few of Big Foot's wild young men, but it never was an objective of the council which was running things. The council's purpose, pure and simple, was to get to Pine Ridge agency where they had friends and relatives, the potential protection of Red Cloud's prestige, and ideally a peacemaking by Chief Big Foot which would give them an extra 100 horses.

The military was conducting a campaign, in short, against the Sioux rebellion—centered primarily in the Oglala and Brulé skirmishes between the White Clay and the Stronghold. Big Foot's headmen, on the other hand, were trying to get out of everybody's gunshot range. But by the very fact of his flight, Big Foot had now identified himself in the military mind as a conspirator of the worst sort—one who must be run down and trapped at all costs.

When Colonel Sumner found that his wards had got away from him and called on Colonel Carr for help, he suggested that the band might be headed straight for the Stronghold. Carr therefore got his squadrons sweeping across the Bad Lands neighborhood and northward, clear to the headwaters of Deep Creek.

Amusingly enough, on this very night that Big Foot's people stopped their frantic chase at last and settled down for a full night's rest on the White River, one of Carr's squadrons commanded by Major Emil Adam was camping only ten miles to the west near the mouth of Red Water Creek. But so obsessed were Major Adam's superiors with the notion that the Stronghold was Big Foot's goal, the cavalry troop was ordered by messenger, just before dawn, to move still farther west and closer to the Stronghold, in order to "intercept" the Minneconjous.

Big Foot's council had so little intention of turning in this direction that they had not even sent scouts up the river, and thus knew nothing of this close brush with white soldiers as Adam's cavalry went galloping away from them.

On this same morning of December 25, it became apparent that Big Foot's health was now a major problem. He was coughing up blood at an alarming rate. He conveyed to his headmen that he wanted messengers sent ahead to Pine Ridge, telling the Indian leaders there that he was on his way. The council immediately dispatched Bear-Comes-and-Lies, Big Voice Thunder and Blue Eagle on this errand.

"Tell them," said Big Foot, "that we come not stealthily, but openly and in peace. Tell them I am very sick."

Big Foot's illness had in fact developed into pneumonia. The travel in his wagon was so wracking to him that the headmen stopped the caravan at a spring only a few miles from the White River, and the band camped there the rest of that day and that night.

The next morning they tried again to move, but again the chief had a fit of coughing so dismaying to the leaders that they stopped after a gain of only four miles, camping on Red Water Creek the night of December 26.

In the middle of the night Big Voice Thunder returned from Pine Ridge. He and his companions had advised the Indian community there of Big Foot's approach, and almost at once, he said, things began to happen. A troop of horse-soldiers had moved out as far as the Wounded Knee trading post and camped there. These soldiers were right now in the Minneconjou band's path if they continued on a direct course to the agency.

Once more Big Foot's headmen were in turmoil. They were still debating the next morning when Bear-Comes-and-Lies also returned, accompanied by an Oglala from the agency named Shaggy Feather. These two had been sent by the Oglala leaders to tell Big Foot that the last of the Stronghold rebels had now given up. Kicking Bear and Short Bull were on their way into the agency at last with all of their followers, and would arrive in two days. It would be strategically advantageous to all the Dakotas, said the Oglala leaders, if Big Foot would plan his arrival on the same day so as to make a show of force. They suggested, therefore, that the Minnecoujous swing east, make a wide circle around the cavalry on Wounded Knee Creek, and come into Pine Ridge from the south.

The assumption that this straggling band could move around the troops without detection was itself naive. A squadron of the 7th Cavalry under Major Samuel Whitside had been sent to Wounded Knee by General Brooke to intercept Big Foot's people, within minutes after the informers in the Indian community at Pine Ridge learned from the Minneconjou messengers where the band was. Whitside now had scouting parties all over the countryside.

But Big Foot himself settled the matter. As sick and weak as he was, he gave an order from his bed in the wagon:

"I am much too sick to spend two more days getting to the agency. It is better that we move directly to where the soldiers are, tell them of our peaceable intentions, and go along with them into Pine Ridge."

By early afternoon the band was on the road again. As painful as the rough wagon ride was for Big Foot, there was no longer time to tarry. They made eight or nine miles by suppertime, crossed Medicine Root Creek after eating, and were well up American Horse Creek by midnight. There they camped, near an abandoned schoolhouse where Little Wound's village had stood only a few weeks earlier.

When the sun came up on December 28, the Minneconjous climbed up out of the American Horse valley and meandered west across the prairie that led to Porcupine Creek. Toward noon, High Hawk and the other warriors riding ahead came to the edge of the prairie and looked down the slope to the creek. At the foot of the hill were four riders watering their horses.

High Hawk signalled his companions to spread out, and they closed in on the strangers. The leader of the four men proved to be Little Bat Garnier, veteran scout, whom many of the Indians knew. With him were his half-brother, Old Hand, and two Oglala scouts, High Backbone and Broken Hammer. After some friendly conversation, the four scouts were taken to Big Foot's wagon, where he lay motionless.

The chief listened to the story and then said feebly, "Let Old Hand and High Backbone go. I want them to ride to the soldiers at Wounded Knee and tell their chief that I am coming in peace. Keep Little Bat and the other one with us until we arrive there."

Old Hand and his companion rode off. The Minneconjou band spread out along the creek and the families ate such lunch as they had. After a while they were ordered back into their wagons and the march continued. They could now see plainly the full length of Porcupine Butte, a steep-sided lump on the landscape with a scattering of scrub pines across its crest. It lay about halfway to Wounded Knee Creek, where they were headed.

Big Foot summoned Red Fish now and said, "You had better send Little Bat and the other one on ahead. We do not want to approach the soldiers with any bad thing on our part."

So the second pair of scouts rode off toward the butte at a gallop. Then Big Foot stopped his wagon and called his headmen around him. He was bleeding from both nose and mouth, and it was painful for him to talk, but some final instructions were imperative.

"Tell our warriors they must not be afraid to go in among the soldiers," he croaked. "Let us all be calm, and show no fear."

He was not at all sure what was going to happen here, but he was determined that they would meet the situation proudly and manfully, neither precipitating trouble nor cowering before the white soldiers.

At his headquarters in Rapid City, General Miles observed that the Sioux rebellion was falling apart, and without realizing it he was somewhat disappointed. He had thought of this grand drama as his own, fully equivalent in romance to the Little Big Horn affair and probably greater. The probability that he would be the hero of it all had crossed his mind repeatedly.

But now word had come that the last of the "hostile" bands in the Stronghold was filing down the slopes toward the agency. Kicking Bear's and Short Bull's warriors had kept up their desultory skirmishing for two weeks, despite an overpowering delegation of "friendlies" whom Brooke had sent up as persuaders. Finally, like Little Wound and Two Strike and all the others before them, the last of the ghost dance leaders had grown tired of the game. They were on their way in to surrender.

The only "hostiles" left at large were Big Foot's band, and it looked as if Brooke would have them cornered shortly.

Like most men reared amid the fantasy and glory of military service, General Miles believed that precise and ruthless orders, executed without hesitation or cavil, were the secret of success. And while he truly believed himself to be the friend and protector of the Indian who had been his charge for so much of his career, his actions reflected in every way the patronizing and superior attitude of the white man toward the "savage" at this period of American history.

It was no longer permissible to say in polite society that the only good Indian was a dead one, but the determination to make the Red Man jump at the white man's every whim was so deep that it was perfectly proper, from the military point of view, to kill off Indians in droves if they "misbehaved," as one would exterminate a mischievous flock of crows or a village of prairie dogs.

This quite conscious contempt for the Red Man was not characteristic of the soldier alone, of course. It was common among the white settlers and fortune hunters, and not uncommon even among the Christian missionaries. A report of the Presbyterian Foreign Mission Board to the Board of Indian Commissioners in this year of 1890 said, quite unblushingly:

"Mr. Sterling's report of the Cheyenne community, in which there are 500 people, is especially interesting. In the services which he has held among these people settled on the White River, there has often been evidence of deep feeling. These poor waifs express their joy at the message of forgiveness, and call upon God in prayer. . . . "

General Miles had grand ambitions for himself, and so he tended to phrase his official pronouncements in somewhat pompous prose which would sound good in the history books, as well as in the newspapers. He did not always realize how revealing they would be to subsequent generations.

For example, on December 1, he declared to the world:

"The conspiracy extends to more different tribes that have heretofore been hostile, but that are now in full sympathy with each other, and are scattered over a larger area of country than in the whole history of Indian warfare."

The whole statement is debatable, but the term "conspiracy" was patently intended to evoke visions of a heinous and well-organized plot. If the Teton Sioux had been capable of such a thing, the "rebellion" would have cost the lives of far more than the two-score soldiers and militiamen which it ultimately took.

"Altogether there are in the Northwest about 30,000 who are affected by the Messiah craze," the general went on. "That means fully 6,000 fighting men. Of this number, fully one-third would not go on the warpath, so that leaves us with about 4,000 adversaries."

These figures were a serious distortion, and Miles should have known it. In the first place, what did he mean by the phrase "affected by the Messiah craze"? Most of the Indians performing the ghost dance were simply swept up in a religious fervor having nothing to do with organized rebellion. Only one-tenth of those who might be said to have been "affected" ever paid any serious attention to it. Many just stood around and watched. In all the bands, there were headmen who opposed the ghost dance throughout the episode. And on some reservations in the area—Crow Creek and Lower Brulé, for example—the dance never got started.

General Miles' effort to scare the country into believing the Sioux had an army of 4,000 fighting men was pathetic, for it fed the nation's craving for excitement and romance at the Indian's bitter expense.

"Four thousand Indians can make an immense amount of trouble," said the general, exploiting his own exaggeration. "Only a tithe of that number were concerned in the Minnesota massacre, yet they killed 500 settlers in a very brief space of time."

The Minnesota massacres by the Santee Sioux a generation earlier, it is true, represented a general uprising by virtually a whole tribe against the white invaders. If the Santees had been half as badly split among themselves as the western Sioux now were, the Minnesota affair would have been contained with far less loss. And the Tetons, although they had scores of opportunities, almost never harmed white civilians and seldom touched their property or livestock.

"The Indians are better armed now than they ever were," the general continued. "And their supply of horses is all that could be desired. Every buck has a Winchester rifle, and he knows how to use it."

An able-bodied Indian male was a "buck" to men of Miles' profession, almost never a "man."

"I hope the problem may be solved without bloodshed," he concluded piously, "but such a happy ending to the trouble seems impossible. . . . "

Given this mental approach to the situation, it is hardly surprising that, when it was all over, General Miles wrote defensively, "These Indians under Big Foot were the most desperate there were. . . . (They) started south for the Bad Lands, evidently intending . . . to go to war. All their movements were intercepted, and their severe loss at the hands of the Seventh Cavalry may be a wholesome lesson to the other Sioux."

Translated into direct orders to his subordinates, the temper of General Miles' attitude produced the following:

After news of Sitting Bull's death—"I have directed the troops to ride down and capture or destroy the few that have escaped from Standing Rock. General Brooke has more than 1,000 lodges or 5,000 Indians under his control at Pine Ridge, but there are still 50 lodges or over 200 fighting men in the Bad Lands that are very defiant and hostile."

December 26, Miles to General Brooke—"Big Foot is cunning and his Indians are very bad. . . ."

December 27, Brooke's aide to Major Whitside—"I am directed by the Commanding General to say that he thinks Big Foot's party must be in front of you somewhere. . . . Find his trail and follow, or find his hiding place and capture him. If he fights, destroy him."

December 28, Miles to Brooke—"Use force enough!"

Colonel James W. Forsyth, who took command of the whole Wounded Knee operation late that night, said his orders were "to disarm Big Foot's band, take every precaution to prevent the escape of any, and if they fought to destroy them."

Destroy them, destroy them, destroy them! Those were the words that set the tone for what was about to happen.

This sentiment inevitably filtered all the way down through the ranks, and virtually all of the troops went at their tasks that night and the next morning, anxious, jumpy and trigger-happy.

Yet General Miles had the gall to call a court of inquiry a week later and try to hang the whole grisly madness on Colonel Forsyth.

When Bear-Comes-and-Lies and the other messengers reached Red Cloud's village at Pine Ridge and began telling their story, the news got to General Brooke's aides in a matter of minutes. So many of the Indians there were on the government's payroll in one way or another that secrecy about anything was virtually impossible.

Major Whitside was ordered out immediately at the head of four troops from Custer's old 7th Cavalry and a platoon of artillery with two Hotchkiss guns. He went straight to the trading post on Wounded Knee Creek. Louis Mousseau, the Wounded Knee storekeeper, who had come into the agency for protection a month earlier, went along to open the store and make his house available as headquarters.

John Shangreau, brother of Louis, was chief of Brooke's headquarter scouts, and he was sent along with Whitside. The next morning his scouts began roaming through the hills looking for Big Foot's trail, but they found nothing that day. The Minneconjou caravan was still twenty miles away, of course, moving slowly toward Medicine Root Creek, and it did not get to the crossing of American Horse Creek, where camp was made, until midnight.

It was the next day, the 28th, that Big Foot's advance riders came upon Little Bat and his companions by surprise. As soon as Old Hand and High Backbone raced the seven miles into Whitside's camp with the news, the major hustled his men into their saddles.

Shangreau objected.

"Look here, Major, aren't you likely to startle them into a fight if you go riding at them? They're coming to us, so why not wait for 'em?"

But Whitside felt the excitement of the chase now, and he was not going to risk failure through any lack of aggressiveness on his part.

"No," he said, "some of our troops or scouts may come upon them and start shooting. I'll go bring them in."

And he signalled his column to move forward.

In an hour they were four miles out, on the east side of Porcupine Butte. The gently rolling prairie revealed nothing, then suddenly there were two horsemen coming over the ridge at full speed. It was Little Bat and Broken Hammer.

Almost before Little Bat had reached Shangreau and the major, Big Foot's column itself began to appear along the ridge.

"How do things look with them up there?" asked Shangreau.

"They look pretty tough," replied Little Bat. "I wouldn't be surprised if we catch it today!"

He was embarrassed about his temporary detention by Big Foot's men, and it relieved him to describe his captors as ferocious.

Whitside ordered his cavalrymen into a skirmish line and had the men dismount. The two Hotchkiss cannons were pulled up in front of the line, and the horses led to the rear. The long line of soldiers prepared for action, most of them lying on their stomachs and checking their rifles.

The warriors who preceded the Minneconjou train were

of course uneasy now, and they kept spreading out as they came. Some stopped and tied up their horses' tails as if for battle. But on Big Foot's wagon behind them, there was a white cloth mounted at the top of a long pole, calling for a peaceful parley.

At a discreet distance, the cavalcade of Indian warriors halted. Two of the men dismounted and walked forward. Shangreau rode out to meet them and shook hands. After a few words he followed them back to Big Foot's wagon.

"*Hau, kola!*" he said to the chief, and shook hands. "Partner, come with me and see the commanding officer."

Big Foot signalled his nephew, who was driving the team, and the wagon moved ahead to Major Whitside astride his mount. The warriors were milling about, unwilling to let their chief get too firmly into the hands of the white men without their protection. They heard the clicking of cartridges into cavalry rifles all around them.

Dewey Horn Cloud threw himself off his horse and, to the astonishment of the Hotchkiss gun crew, thrust a hand into the cannon to show them that he had no fear of them or their weapons.

Someone laid back the blanket that covered Big Foot's upper body and Major Whitside saw the pitiful figure with whom he must deal.

"Are you able to talk?" he asked tentatively, with Shangreau interpreting.

"*Hau,*" replied Big Foot, and he raised his arm feebly to shake hands.

"I heard that you came out of Cheyenne River as a war party, and I've been looking for you. Where are you going?"

"I want to see my people on White Clay Creek, so I'm going to the agency."

"Well, I'm glad to find you peaceful. Why do you want to go to the agency?"

Big Foot tried to clear his hoarse throat. "Because they sent for me. They want me to make a peace and I will get a hundred horses."

The major smiled. "All right, but I want you to come on into Wounded Knee and camp there."

"That is good," mumbled the chief, "I was going down there."

Remembering his orders, Whitside turned to his interpreter and said, "John, I want their horses and guns!"

"Oh, wait a minute, Major!" said Shangreau firmly. "If you do that you're liable to have a fight right here, and if that happens you'll kill all these women and children while the men get away from us!"

"But you know what Brooke's orders are: *Dismount and disarm!*"

Shangreau stood his ground. "I can't help it. If we expect to disarm them, we'd better take them to camp first, and then get their horses and guns."

Whitside was torn for a few seconds. Then he said, "All right, tell Big Foot to come on down to Wounded Knee and camp."

The chief had been watching the two men, uncertain what the discussion was about. The cavalry officer reached out to shake hands with him again, glancing hesitantly at the bloody mouth. Then he turned back to Shangreau.

"John, that's an awful thing for him to ride in. Let's get him into an ambulance." And his aides signalled for an ambulance wagon to be brought up.

"My father," said Shangreau to the chief, "they are going to put you in a better wagon, and the soldier chief wants all your people to come on down to Wounded Knee and camp there."

"*Hau,*" replied Big Foot, "I intend to camp there. That is where we are going."

Soldiers from the ambulance unit lifted Big Foot carefully on his blankets into the other vehicle, the cavalry mounted up, and the train started southwestward. Two troops of cavalry led the procession. The other two troops herded the wagons on behind, signalled the warriors to fall in, and then brought up the rear.

Whitside rushed a courier off to the nearest heliograph, a string of which had been set up along the hilltops to keep them in constant touch with General Brooke and the agency. In a few minutes the mirrors were flashing the news through the late afternoon sunlight that Big Foot's band had been intercepted and had surrendered.

The major suggested to his superiors that Colonel Forsyth and the rest of the 7th Calvary be sent to Wounded Knee to help disarm the Indians. By this time it had got through his head that taking the guns and horses away from these warriors might not be any Sunday school picnic.

At Pine Ridge, General Brooke ordered Forsyth out at once. As soon as the band was disarmed, he said in a wire to General Miles, the prisoners would be marched to the railroad in Nebraska and shipped to Omaha for "further disposition."

It was almost dark when Colonel Forsyth left Pine Ridge with his four troops of cavalry, a troop of Oglala scouts, another platoon of artillery with two Hotchkiss guns, and a string of supply wagons. About the same time, Major Whitside's "prisoners" were crossing the rude bridge over Wounded Knee Creek and turning into a broad, flat meadow between the cavalry camp and a dry ravine beyond. Some of the Indians stopped at Mousseau's store to buy coffee, sugar, candles, bacon and other supplies.

When he went out to Porcupine Butte earlier in the day, Whitside had ordered a camp detail to set up a row of white duck tents that had been brought along from the agency.

"When we bring these redskins in," he had said, "I want shelter for them where we can keep an eye on them. String the tents along here south of the enlisted men's tents, but leave an opening so the sentries can stand through there."

Peter McFarland, a civilian freighter who had brought a load of supplies, erected two larger canvas tents for the scouts and teamsters first, and then had workmen raise the cluster of smaller tents.

But when the Minneconjous began to stream down from the creek bridge, even those without shelter of their own would not stop at the tents offered them. They did not care to have armed white men so close behind them, and they moved on down toward the ravine instead. All of them were accommodated one way or another among their own tepees.

It was a significant token of the Minneconjous' essentially peaceful intentions that nothing untoward happened when they were separated from their horses. Whitside had ordered a chain guard around the camp, the horses to be staked outside of it and farther down the ravine. "Don't let the bucks through the guard," he said. "Let the little kids stake out the horses."

And so as one family after another came to the sentries at the chain, the soldiers shook their heads and pointed to one of the little boys. The warrior or his wife would hand the tether rope to a youngster, and the soldier would lift the chain and allow the boy and ponies to pass outside. Not a single Indian raised more than an amused objection to this procedure.

When the soldiers finally had the camp more or less settled, there had arisen some eighty tepees in an arc about 800 feet long and 400 feet across its center. The heavy smell of wood smoke and cooking food soon filled the still, cold air.

Major Whitside had had Chief Big Foot put into one of McFarland's large tents, and a camp stove installed in it for warmth. McFarland spread his buffalo coat on a cot for the chief to lie on, and Little Bat was kept there as an interpreter while a surgeon treated Big Foot as best he could, seeking to reduce the sick man's discomfort. Mrs. Big Foot stayed at one side whenever the surgeon was there ministering to her husband.

The two Hotchkiss guns were hauled to the top of a small hill overlooking the Indian camp and were aimed directly at it. Troops A and I were stationed so as to encircle the Indians completely, with twenty posts between which sentries moved during the night.

Late in the evening Colonel Forsyth and his troops arrived from Pine Ridge, and he took over command. They had come with a minimum of baggage and bivouacked on the opposite side of Whitside's camp from the Indian village.

Forsyth added his two Hotchkiss guns to those already on the hill. The troop of Oglala scouts camped in a line along the ravine across from Big Foot's people, just beyond the row of sentry stations.

There were more than 200 Indian women and children and old men in this encampment, and just over 100 young or adult males. They were now surrounded by some 500 white soldiers and Indian Army scouts.

Colonel Forsyth had circled his troops south and east of the camp before marching in, hoping not to be noticed in the dark amongst Whitside's troops. But the minute the Oglala scouts turned in across the ravine, the Minneconjous heard the Sioux chatter and called to their cousins. In short order the whole Indian camp knew the size and character of Forsyth's additions to the white fighting force.

But no matter, for it was Whitside's intent, when he asked for Forsyth's help, to so overawe the Minneconjous that they would meekly surrender their arms and the ponies on which they might otherwise try to escape.

Big Foot's warriors were worried, all right, but not altogether as resigned to abject surrender as Whitside hoped.

The 7th Cavalry officers, however, felt that the little campaign was as good as over. James Asay, a trader at Pine Ridge, had come along with Forsyth's outfit hauling a barrel of whisky, and there were sounds of toasting and gaiety from the officers' tents until late in the night.

When the Minneconjou men learned that more than twice the original number of soldiers now surrounded them, many of them declined to go to bed at all, lest the white troops planned an attack on them during the night. A number of them hovered in the vicinity of Big Foot's tent. The chief himself was so near unconsciousness that he scarcely knew what was going on. Some of the watchful warriors stepped into his tent now and then, and they would visit briefly with Little Bat. The scout sought to reassure them that there was no reason for apprehension, but he realized that he was not succeeding very well. Then he discovered that twenty or more of the Oglala scouts had disappeared, apparently fearing trouble and not wishing to participate in any bloodshed at the expense of their brothers, the Minneconjous.

This worried Little Bat.

CHAPTER V

THE KILLING

As daylight came to the rolling prairie along Wounded Knee Creek on the cold morning of December 29, Chief Big Foot lay huddled in his greatcoat and blankets on the Army cot. Beside him sat his wife on a buffalo robe which one of the freight-haulers had thrown down for her comfort. The chief stirred uneasily and she watched his face to see whether she would only awaken him if she wiped the trickles of blood from around his nose and mouth.

The ground around them was covered with the winter's colorless, dry grass. One could hear plainly the tramping back and forth of many feet outside on the frozen soil and the jumble of voices as the soldiers performed their duties. Horses whinnied in the distance, and now and then a mule brayed. There was talking in the white man's language, but Mrs. Big Foot understood none of it.

Somewhat farther away arose the noises of an Indian camp making breakfast. Sometimes a child squealed as he chased a companion among the tepees.

Chief Big Foot opened his eyes and mumbled some words. The woman dug a cloth out of her possessions, dipped it in a pan of water at her side, and held it against his forehead for a minute. Then she rolled it into a soft band, wetted it again, and lifted his shaggy head so as to slip it under his temple, tying its ends at the back of his head.

As the clamor outside increased, the sun's rays appeared on the east side of the tent. Little Bat stopped in with a tin pail of hot coffee and some cold meat, and when Mrs. Big Foot indicated that the sick man would have no interest in it, Little Bat motioned that she herself should eat it. Then he left to resume his services to the Army officers outside.

A few minutes later the elder Horn Cloud entered the tent, looking backward at the scene around him for several seconds before closing the tentflap. (His Siouan name meant Horned Cloud, but the educated sons had found that form too clumsy in English, and dropped the *ed.*) He made a sign asking about the chief, and the woman indicated that nothing had changed. He could see that conversation with Big Foot was inappropriate if not impossible, so he turned and left.

The senior Horn Cloud was worried. The climate in the camp was all wrong. It was the attitude of some of the warriors that disturbed him, as much as the behavior of the white troops. He had taken the unusual step, just before daybreak, of moving among the tepees that housed his sons and their families, touching the adult males noiselessly. Some of the men had stayed awake most of the night, uneasy because of the cannon they had seen positioned on the hill and aimed at their camp. The ones who had been aroused got to their feet and followed Horn Cloud quietly to his own quarters. In the group were William and Sherman, Dewey (who later took the surname Beard), White Lance, young Joseph and teen-age Frank.

The father spoke in a low voice. "I have to tell you truthfully that I do not much like the looks of things here, my sons, and I want to give you some advice. If any of our brothers try to start trouble, do not join in with them. Of course if the white soldiers start shooting, you will do whatever you have to do. In that case, my dear sons, stand together soberly in front of your old folks and little ones, protecting them as long as you can. And if any of you die in this fashion I will be satisfied. But let us not get panicky, whatever happens. If one or two of our men start trouble, they will be arrested and put in jail, and I do not want any of my sons to get into such a useless mess. So stay calm—

unless we should be attacked by soldiers. Then you must defend yourselves and all of us."

He made a sign and the men filed back through the darkness to their tepees. . . .

Now as Horn Cloud left Big Foot's tent, a loud voice was suddenly heard, off in the Indian camp. It was Wounded Hand, calling out:

"There is to be a council with the white soldier chiefs! All warriors come forward and form a circle. . . ."

Mrs. Big Foot heard the words, and since her husband seemed to be asleep, she arose and stepped outside the tent opening. Some distance at one side of the guard ring of the soldiers she saw a white officer talking earnestly to a group of his men. She did not know him, but it was Colonel Forsyth, now in command.

She looked at the circle of Indians now forming in front of the tent, most of them seated cross-legged. Then, embarrassed lest the white officers had seen her gaping, she ducked back into the tent.

Colonel Forsyth had been directing his officers as to the positions the various troops were to take. Troops A and I, which had been standing guard all night in a ring encircling the Indian village, were still there. Big Foot's tent and the now forming council were inside the ring on its north side, halfway between the ravine and the hill where the Hotchkiss guns stood.

Troops B and K were stationed in the military camp streets, 300 feet away, awaiting call. The other four troops, mounted, took positions in the background— Troop E beside the hill where the cannons were, Troop G opposite them on the east toward the creek, C and D strung along behind the row of Indian scouts on the slope across the ravine.

Big Foot's band was surely in a tight and impenetrable

bag, thought Forsyth. No man in his right mind would break out of such a ring unless he was determined to die in the attempt. He summoned his subordinates now and made a brief talk:

"Now, gentlemen, getting their guns away from these bucks may be a little touchy, and I want it perfectly understood what our orders are. We are going to disarm these Indians, and we are ordered to prevent the escape of any of them. If they fight, we are to destroy them. Big Foot's bunch have made fools of us long enough, and I don't intend to let them get away with it here. If there is any firing on their part, I want your men to shoot. Is that clear?"

The men nodded. They knew the rules, and there was nothing more to say. They turned away, each one going to his post.

Colonel Forsyth entered the circle of Indians and stopped short.

"What are these young boys doing here?" he demanded.

Little Bat translated the question to the headmen and then turned back to Forsyth.

"They say these are brave boys, and it is an Indian custom to allow them to sit in council if their fathers wish."

"All right, leave them then," said Forsyth, annoyed. The Indians weren't taking this very seriously, he thought, but after all, there is overwhelmingly superior force here against them and apparently they recognize it. That's all to the good.

Nevertheless, he was somewhat on edge. Getting the Indian men together was proving a maddeningly disorderly business, something he had not anticipated. The first couple of dozen Minneconjous to arrive at the circle after Wounded Hand's call stalled around there for a few minutes and then, restless and uncertain what they were supposed to do, wandered back to the tepee village. But finally most of them drifted in again and it appeared to Shangreau and the officers that they had all the warriors at the council site.

The military force around the Indians had some weaknesses, to be sure. More than eighty of the cavalrymen were inexperienced recruits. In fact, almost half of these had joined the regiment only two weeks earlier at Pine Ridge. Nor could the Oglala scouts be relied upon to put up much of a fight, but so ample was the cavalry that this question did not arise in any officer's mind.

The thing that bothered the soldiers more than any other was that they were equipped with one-shot Springfield rifles. They could not help seeing the day before that many of the Indians had the latest Winchester repeaters, bought more or less freely from white traders throughout the West—frequently at exorbitant prices, of course.

When at last everything seemed to be ready, Colonel Forsyth began to speak in a loud tone so that everyone would know he was saying something important. He waited every sentence or two for Shangreau to translate.

"I want to assure you Minneconjous that you and your people are perfectly safe under the protection of your old friends, the soldiers. All of your troubles are coming to an end. We will not let you starve any more, but will feed you well.

"However, in order to be sure there is no trouble of any kind, I must ask you to turn in your guns to me, and then we will go along to the agency."

Of course many of the older Indians had anticipated this announcement. It was a demand that had been made of them before in similar situations. But it was especially resented by the young radicals, who were in no mood to acquiesce in the white soldiers' every whim anyway. The Indian's gun was his most prized possession—more important, somehow, even than his horse. It was a supreme weapon with which to defend himself and his family, both in battle and in the struggle for food.

When the translation fell from Shangreau's lips, there was a sudden silence so deep that the cavalry horses could be heard stomping on the hillside, the children laughing and playing at the Indian camp. The short silence was followed by an eruption of angry words among the young warriors.

Forsyth and Whitside waited a moment, uncertain how to proceed. Then High Hawk stepped forward and said to Shangreau, "We want to talk to our chief."

Shangreau repeated the request to the colonel, and Forsyth said, "Tell them to go ahead."

High Hawk and another headman walked over to Big Foot's tent, followed by Shangreau. High Hawk knelt beside his chief, who was unable to turn his head upward.

"Father, they want to take our guns away from us. We will do whatever you say."

The sick man tried to clear his brain. Let's see, where are we now? Have we moved along while I was sleeping? No, I guess not. We're still out on the open prairie.

He started mumbling, his words rattling in his dry throat. "This is the third time they have tried to take the guns away from me. I'll tell you what: You give them the bad guns and keep the good ones!"

Shangreau smelled trouble. It seemed clear to him that the ailing chief was confused and did not realize the implications of such a decision.

"Wait a minute, my friends," he interrupted, speaking to High Hawk rather than the chief. "You had better give up the guns. If you give them up, you can get others later on. You can buy them. But if you lose a man, you cannot buy another in his place."

Big Foot heard the admonition and spoke again, so softly the words were barely audible.

"No, we will keep the good guns."

The two Indians walked out of the tent as Shangreau
stood looking helplessly first at Big Foot and then at his
wife.

When the scout returned to Forsyth and reported on
the conference, the colonel spoke angrily. "All right, let's
break them into smaller groups and get started here.
Major, count off twenty men and send them to their camp
for their guns. I want them brought back here. John will
talk for you."

Shangreau and Major Whitside counted off twenty Indians and sent them to their tepee village. While they
were gone, the larger group became restless again and
somewhat noisy. Some arose and went unbidden to their
camp. Dewey Horn Cloud took advantage of the confusion to dig shallow trenches behind his tepee and bury
both his gun and his extra ammunition. Then he kicked
horse manure over the trenches to conceal them.

After a considerable wait, the warriors came straggling
back to the council circle. Only two of them brought
guns—old, broken weapons which obviously had not
been used recently.

Whitside was nervous and losing his temper. "This
won't do," he said to the colonel. "Let's get Big Foot out
here and see that he gives his men the proper orders."

Forsyth agreed, and a soldier and several Indians were
sent into the tent to carry the chief out. They motioned
Mrs. Big Foot to one side and spread a heavy blanket on
the ground beside the invalid. Then they lifted him from
his cot onto the blanket.

Big Foot looked at the men rather stupidly as they
moved him, puzzled about what was happening, but he

made no protest. When he was carried out the door of the tent he squinted into the sky and tried to move, but Courage Bear and the senior Horn Cloud stepped forward and laid their hands gently on his shoulders, saying, "It's all right, Father, just lie still." Frog and old Wounded Hand also hovered protectively around him. In spite of the traces of blood at the chief's nose and mouth, his wife had remained inside the tent as was proper.

Shangreau was now busy across the council circle translating officers' orders to the warriors, so Colonel Forsyth summoned Interpreter Philip Wells forward to talk to Big Foot.

"Tell the chief that I want him to tell the men to surrender their guns."

The sick man opened his eyes and mumbled a reply. Wells leaned over to listen and then turned to Forsyth.

"He says the ones you have found are all they have. He says their guns were all gathered up at the Cheyenne agency and burned."

Forsyth was furious. "You tell Big Foot he claims his Indians have no guns, yet yesterday at the time of their surrender they were all well armed! He is plainly deceiving me. Tell him he needn't have any fear about giving up the arms, because I wish to treat him with nothing but kindness."

He waited for the translation, but the chief was silent and showed no sign of cooperating.

The officer now bent down directly over Big Foot's crumpled form.

"Have I not done enough to convince you that I intend nothing but good treatment?"

His tone was showing his frustration.

"Did we not put you in an ambulance and treat you kindly, and put you in a good tent, and put a stove in it to keep you warm and comfortable? And I have sent back for provisions for your people which I expect to arrive at any time, so that I can feed you well. And I have had my doctor taking care of you. . . ."

Forsyth stood up, exasperated.

Wells translated his last remarks and then looked up at the commander. "He says thay haven't any more guns."

"He is lying to me in return for all my kindnesses," snapped Forsyth. "You tell him that!"

Big Foot neither moved nor responded. Consciousness was slowly slipping away again. He was exhausted even to the limits of his sturdy frame. To whatever degree he understood now what was going on, he could not find it in his heart to leave his people naked before the caprices and the vastly superior armor of these white soldiers as perhaps his last official act.

Forsyth turned away angrily and Whitside said, "Well, at least we can stop this traffic back and forth to their camp. It's demoralizing the whole business."

It was true that a few of the Indians had brought additional guns back to the circle, but they were mostly broken or badly worn, some even tied together with string.

"That's a good idea," said Forsyth, and an order was given to bring B and K troops inside the guard ring from the soldiers' camp. As the men came down, some of the newer recruits attempted to cover their uneasiness with light banter and bravado.

"You don't s'pose these goddam redskins will actually try to break, do you?" a boyish soldier asked of no one in particular.

"Well, if they do," a companion responded, "they'll sure get their asses full of lead, and that'll slow down their getaway!"

There was a low tittering and a trooper several paces behind, muttered *sotto voce*, "What the hell do you think

I joined Custer's outfit for? Just give us an excuse to get at 'em!"

Captain George Wallace now lined his Troop K behind the council circle on the south, and Captain Charles Varnum's Troop B stood at right angles on the west. The 110 soldiers were only a few paces from the cluster of Indians, and they effectively blocked the path to the Indian camp.

Forsyth realized that he was not going to get what he wanted by voluntary action on the part of the warriors.

"Where's Shangreau?" he asked, looking around him.

The interpreter stepped forward.

"John, I want you to go with a detail of Captain Wallace's men and start searching from the east end of the Indian camp. I want their guns, and you may have to dig for them. We'll keep the bucks here. . . . Captain Varnum, take fifteen of your men and start searching from the hill. Take Little Bat with you. He and John will explain to the squaws what you're doing."

Within a minute the two search parties were gone, and occasional squeals and cries of protest began emanating from the village. But for the most part, the women were silent and ignored the intruders.

The two captains, their lieutenants and a couple of sergeants did the searching inside the tepees, while the privates stood guard outside. At one tepee an Indian woman was sitting on the ground rather awkwardly, her skirts spread out around her.

"Move her," said a sergeant, and a soldier took her arm and pulled her to one side. The sergeant picked up the bright Winchester that had been under her.

When several guns had been uncovered in this way, it became obvious that the Indians—men and women alike—had been ingenious in their methods of concealment, and the officers at both ends of the camp started searching more deeply within the tepees. Large bundles were suspect, and were cut open. If knives or hatchets were discovered, they were considered weapons and were thrown out into the growing pile guarded by the soldiers.

Around the camp stood numerous wagons already packed for resumption of the march to Pine Ridge. Now the soldiers began throwing all suspicious bundles out of the wagons. Rolls of clothing and bedding were cut or burst open, and occasionally a concealed gun was found and added to the pile.

Some soldiers from the hill nearby were called to start carrying the collected weapons to the circle where the colonel and major were. The accumulation contained some war clubs, a few axes and some bows and arrows, as well as guns.

As a soldier emptied one bundle of cooking utensils and started to carry off the knives, the Indian woman screamed to Shangreau in Siouan, "How can I feed my family if I am robbed in this way?"

The interpreter took the knives from the soldier's arms and handed them back to her. Then he gave her some crackers from his pocket.

The little children, unaware of the significance of what was going on, continued to romp and play around the tents, and Captain Wallace stopped occasionally to give one of them a friendly chuck under the chin.

But things were not quiet at the council circle during this hour or more. The younger warriors milled around and complained loudly among themselves.

Yellow Bird, the medicine man, arose and began a little dance, moving slowly around the circle and singing softly. The officers paid little attention to it at first because they were preoccupied with other things. Now and then Yellow Bird stomped, raised his hands high in the air, and uttered some kind of prayer.

"What's he saying?" Forsyth finally asked Interpreter Wells.

"I think it's only a harmless prayer, Colonel, but I'll listen for a minute and tell you if it's important."

Forsyth accepted this assurance and walked away.

Yellow Bird stooped down and scraped up some of the dusty yellow soil in his hands. Then, sweeping his arms in a symbolic arc over the soldiers standing guard, he loosed the dirt and it drifted away in the light breeze. He continued his dance steps all the way around the circle of Indians, and when he returned to his starting place he intoned a Sioux prayer of commitment:

"It is too bad I must do this, but I now take a desperate course. I have submitted to abuse, insult, and wrong with great patience and fortitude. If now I have determined to retaliate and take my revenge upon those who have done these wrongs to me, well—ha! ha! ha!—I have lived long enough!"

Wells had heard enough to be made distinctly uneasy. He looked for Forsyth. Yellow Bird started moving around the circle again, this time dropping off his blanket. Wells saw that he was wearing only a ghost-shirt, breech-cloth and leggings. Parts of his body were painted blue with yellow spots—ghost dance symbols.

By this time Wallace and Varnum had at last finished their search of the entire Indian camp and had returned to the council circle, their details resuming their posts. They had collected 38 rifles, a few of which were Winchesters. Forsyth and Whitside were sure this wasn't all of them.

"I know damned well they have them under their blankets," said the major, "and we'd better get them pronto!"

"Philip," Colonel Forsyth called to Wells, who was on his way over there. "Tell these bucks that we're going to search them, two or three at a time. Tell them I didn't want to do it this way, but I will have to unless they come forward like men and lay down their guns."

Wells made the short speech and several of the older Indians, led by Frog, moved toward the center, opening their blankets to show that they had no guns and saying, *"Hau! Hau!"* to encourage the cooperation of the younger men.

The young warriors, however, at first hung back and then began to move away slowly toward the far side of the circle. Yellow Bird started an exhortation to them:

"Warriors! Do not be afraid! Let your hearts be strong to meet the test that is now before you. There are soldiers all about us and they have lots of bullets. But I have received assurances that their bullets cannot penetrate us! The prairie is large, and the bullets will go over you into the prairie! Just as you saw my dust drift away, so will the bullets drift away harmlessly!"

Several of the young warriors cried *"Hau! Hau!"* in approval.

By this time Wells had got back around the circle to Iron Eyes, Big Foot's brother-in-law, and said to him, "My friend, won't you go over there and quiet Yellow Bird and the young men? Talk to them as a man of your age should."

The Indian responded with sarcasm, "Why, friend, your heart is pounding! Why? Who talks of making trouble here?"

Forsyth called across to his interpreter, "Wells, you'd better get out of there. It's getting a bit touchy."

"I will in a minute, Colonel. I want to see if I can't get this fellow to quiet them."

And turning back to Iron Eyes, Wells resumed the Sioux language: "Yes, my friend, my heart beats hard when I see so many helpless women and children nearby—" he motioned toward the village. "If anything should happen here—"

But the headman interrupted him in a loud, sneering voice. "Friend, it is not necessary for your heart to beat so fast!"

The interpreter walked back quickly to Forsyth and Whitside and told them what Yellow Bird seemed to be saying to the young men. The colonel then went with Wells to the medicine man and ordered him to sit down on the ground and be quiet.

"He'll sit down when he gets around the circle," said Iron Eyes insolently to Wells. "Tell the soldier chief that our Big Foot is dying and we wish to continue our journey to Pine Ridge without further foolishness!"

Wells translated, and Forsyth turned angrily to Iron Eyes. "I can take better care of him than you can anywhere. I have doctors tending to him."

Yellow Bird finally squatted down, and Forsyth returned to Whitside and the search for concealed weapons. The young warriors crowded ever more tightly together, their blankets around them. A sergeant said excitedly, "Colonel, sir, there's one with a gun under his blanket!"

The Indian, apart from the others, was pulled over and his rifle jerked from him. A nervous young cavalryman, watching the drama unfold from a few rods off, was muttering half to himself, "Holy Christ, Colonel, you've stretched this thing as tight as a banjo string already! Something's going to snap unless you ease off. . . . What the hell harm can it do if the last half dozen of them still have rifles? They can't hurt us now!"

But the officer was thinking only of the order, *"Disarm them!"* and the search went on. One at a time the sheets were pulled from the sullen warriors.

Lieutenant James Mann walked up and down before Captain Wallace's troop saying in a low voice, "Be ready, men! There's going to be trouble!"

The soldiers kept their guns pointed at the crowd of Indians, and their nervousness put most of them in a slightly crouching stance.

Black Coyote was stomping around holding his rifle high in the air now with both hands. The officers learned afterward that he was quite deaf, but few of the people here were aware of it. He had misunderstood something one of the interpreters had said, and he was declaring angrily to the other warriors that he, Black Coyote, was not going to stand still while anybody held a gun to his head and pulled the trigger, even if it was not loaded. The Indians who heard this thought Black Coyote had come upon some secret information, and that when they had given up their guns they would be lined up and subjected to this indignity in order to humble them. Some even suggested it was a trick, and that the guns would indeed have cartridges in them so the warriors would all be killed simultaneously.

The senior Horn Cloud arose quickly when he got wind of this nonsense, and looked for an interpreter to tell Colonel Forsyth that he would put Black Coyote straight about the matter. He turned frantically here and there but could find neither Wells nor Shangreau, and now the disturbed Black Coyote was yelling and there was confusion everywhere.

"I paid much money for this gun and it belongs to me!" Black Coyote screamed. "I will not give it up unless I am paid for it in return!"

Two cavalrymen, who had no idea what he was saying, grabbed him from behind. The gun was pointed upward and it went off.

The "banjo string" had snapped.

The half dozen warriors who still had avoided search threw off their blankets and exposed their rifles. Lieutenant W. W. Robinson, adjutant of the Second Squadron, wheeled his horse away and shouted, "Look out, men! Look out! They're going to fire!"

Lieutenant Mann roared, "Fire at them, men! Fire!"

All of the Indian survivors spoke afterward of "the crash." As far as anyone could tell or recall, the six Indian rifles and the weapons of a hundred cavalrymen exploded at the same moment.

When Black Coyote's gun went off, Chief Big Foot made an instinctive move to raise himself. Frog, who had been sitting protectively beside his chief with a blanket over his head for warmth, made a quick gesture to help Big Foot and then rose to his feet, along with a dozen Indians around him. He was hit in the first volley from the soldiers and pitched forward to the ground, where he lay still.

A bullet from the same fusillade struck Chief Big Foot as he fell back, his head bumping clumsily on the frozen ground. Mrs. Big Foot dashed out of the tent and threw herself over his body. A cloud of smoke and dust enveloped and blinded everyone, but a cavalryman with a rifle in one hand and a pistol in the other stepped out of the haze, pointed the pistol at the back of Mrs. Big Foot's head and fired. As her body rolled lazily to one side, he put the pistol back in its holster, shifted his rifle to his right arm, and fired it directly into Big Foot's chest.

There were perhaps fifty Indians in the council circle either killed or immobilized by the soldiers' first volley. The half-dozen young warriors still possessing guns pumped their Winchesters into the lines of troops, and soldiers dropped right and left for a few seconds. The cavalrymen were firing in such a panic that they were shooting into their own comrades on the opposite side of the ring, and even the scouts across the ravine were scurrying for cover.

Father Horn Cloud was killed there in the circle almost immediately, as was his son Sherman. Shedding Bear died there, and High Hawk and He Crow and Crazy Bear and many others—Red Fish, Pretty Hawk, Bear Cuts Body, Black Coyote, Shakes Bird, Charge At Them, Yellow Robe. . . .

Those Indians who were not struck down in the first few seconds plunged recklessly to the pile of rifles, which now numbered over fifty, or grabbed up stone war clubs or hatchets—anything with which to fight. And some of them reached the lines of soldiers while the latter were reloading their Springfields, so that there were a half dozen hand-to-hand contests to the death going on.

The smoke of the shooting and the dust raised by the melee left everyone, white and red, coughing and choking in a suffocating cloud. Captain Wallace ran to his troop at the first shot, but the top of his head was torn off by a bullet almost at once.

Many Indian women in the village, when they heard the "crash" and realized what was happening, seized their children and ran for the ravine in the hope of getting below the gunfire. The bullets ripping through the camp and across the ravine were hitting animals as well as humans, and several teams of horses and mules ran away, pulling their wagons behind them. Some of the wagons tipped over and went plowing through tents and tepees.

Now the mounted troops higher on the slope began firing into the Minneconjous as they came running toward the ditch. The smoke was heavy and there was bedlam everywhere, so that it was hard to distinguish friend from foe. An officer tried to prevent firing into the women and children at first, as they came to the ravine, but a few minutes later he cried, "Here come the bucks! Let 'em have it!" There were still as many women in the crowd, dragging their flocks, as there were warriors, however.

The swarm of humans disappeared for a minute or two as they crossed the bottom of the draw, then they began boiling up the south bank of the ravine toward the agency road. A few were riding ponies they had got hold of, two or three children sometimes hanging on to the clothing of a rider. The camp's dogs ran alongside, trying to follow their masters. Now the cavalrymen of Troops C and D on the south slope loosed a murderous fire upon everything that showed up above the ravine's edge. In four minutes, not a thing was moving on the open flat. There was nothing but dead warriors, dead ponies, dead women and children, dead dogs. Captain Edward Godfrey of Troop D ran his eyes across the smoking field and counted thirty human bodies.

When the shooting started, Dewey Horn Cloud had dived at a trooper to wrench his rifle from him. The soldier fought gamely, and Dewey jerked his hidden long knife from his belt and stabbed his opponent in the breast. The gun dropped, but the soldier grabbed Dewey by the throat and hung on, screaming into the smoke and racket

for someone to help him. They fell to the ground and
Dewey straddled his victim, switching his attack to the
man's side and stabbing repeatedly. The soldier continued
to struggle, and Dewey muttered to himself, "Why
doesn't this miserable man die?"

Gradually the cavalryman's hands loosened on the Indian's throat and Dewey leaped to his feet. He seized the
gun from the ground and ran through the thick clouds of
dust and smoke toward the ravine. On the way he was
shot in the neck and again in the leg. He almost ran into
an officer in the blinding haze, and hesitated long enough
to shoot him.

Dewey dropped over the side of the ravine and lay still
for a moment. There was a roar of shooting all about him.
He fired at a soldier whenever he spotted one. There were
dead or injured women and children here and there, and
it created a terrible anger in his breast. "If I could kill
every white man here," he said to himself, "my hate
would not be satisfied." When he ran out of cartridges, he
began sliding cautiously up the ditch. Shortly he came
upon an elderly wounded Indian who handed over his
gun. Dewey realized he was growing weak from the loss
of blood. Suddenly he saw a group of women coming
down the ravine wailing, with a herd of little boys and
girls in tow. Soldiers were firing at them from the edges of
the ravine, and most of them fell before they passed the
place where Dewey was hiding. One young girl, wounded in the chin and shoulder, lay on the ground crying softly in Siouan, "Mother! Mother!"

Dewey continued to drag himself down the ravine,
shielded by its steep side. He was stunned to see his own
mother stumbling toward him, badly wounded, with a
soldier's pistol in her hand. When she recognized Dewey,
signalling frantically to her to come closer, she cried out,

"No, my son, pass me by quickly! I am going to fall down now!" Those were her last words. A few rods behind her lay Dewey's sister Pretty Enemy, mortally wounded.

He continued crawling along the ravine's side, hiding in the sparse brush as much as possible. But he realized that to escape the battleground, he must get to the other side. His right arm had ceased to be useful, the bullet in his neck having hit the collarbone and traveled down his back and out through the buttock. The arm dangled and flopped against his knees as he crouched to run, so he stuck its thumb in his mouth and held it with his teeth. Then, in a hail of bullets, he streaked across the ravine and had rested there in a gully only a few minutes when White Lance came rolling into the depression, half-dragged and half-carried by George Shoots-the-Bear. Lance had been shot twice. With them was William Horn Cloud, Dewey's brother, blood gushing from a wound in his chest. They lay there panting, trying to decide what to do next. Several wounded persons could be heard singing death chants around them. Dewey was growing steadily weaker, and he said to his companions, "I am unable to do anything more because of my wounds, so I prepare to rest. My brothers, keep up your courage."

The Hotchkiss cannons on the hill had been firing into the Indian village for some time. Many of the women and children had cowered in their tepees, not knowing how to escape. Their shelters were soon blown to bits, and everything combustible set afire. After a half hour there was nothing visible in the smoky haze but occasional bare tepee poles, wrecked wagons and bodies. It was here that Dewey's wife, Wears Eagle, and their small son Tommy had been killed. Later, when Wears Eagle's body was found, their 25-day-old daughter Wet Feet was still trying to nurse at the wound in her mother's breast, and she died three months later.

Three soldiers' bodies were also lying amid the
wreckage of the Indian camp, but Major Whitside
testified at a subsequent hearing that they had been there
"without authority."

Bear Woman, the oldest Minneconjou in the band, was
dead there. So were the wives of High Hawk and Red Fish
and Pretty Hawk and Iron Eyes and Strong Fox and Swift
Bird and many others. So were the mothers of Charge At
Them and Brown Turtle. . . .

After most of the Indians still alive had got into the
ravine, and were either running or dug in somewhere,
several artillerymen ran one of the Hotchkiss guns down
off the hill to a knoll farther west, close enough to the
ravine to wipe out pockets of resistance. After a few pin-
pointed shots, the ravine grew quiet.

Some of the last Hotchkiss shells picked off a
wagon that was trying to escape from the ravine, two
Indians on the ground whipping the horses furiously to
make them climb the south bank. When the shells hit,
women and children and pieces of wagon flew in all
directions.

Forsyth now sent a mounted troop down the ravine
to clean up. Dewey Horn Cloud and his companions
saw them coming and made a dash up a side gully—
all but William Horn Cloud, who had died there of
his chest wound. Somehow the group got clear of the
battle area and ran into young Joseph Horn Cloud,
who had captured a horse and was looking hopefully
for members of his family. He put the blood-spattered
Dewey on the horse and tried to help George Shoots-
the-Bear keep the wounded White Lance on his feet.
They kept well away from the agency road and staggered
into the Holy Rosary Mission toward morning.

During the first few minutes of the fighting, Philip Wells also was engaged in his own private war. As the incident with Iron Eyes was ending, Wells had noticed a powerfully built young warrior intently eyeing his gun, which he held by the muzzle with the stock to the ground. The Indian moved slowly around the circle toward Wells' rear, but the interpreter kept shifting his body so as to keep the warrior in view.

When "the crash" came, the skulker whipped out a huge, pointed knife from his belt and leaped at Wells. The scout threw up his rifle in both hands to ward off the blow as he fell backward. The rifle broke the plunge of the Indian's arm, but the honed point of the knife sliced almost through Wells' nose, so that for the rest of the battle it hung by only a slender piece of flesh.

The Indian came on again and Wells, now on his back, kicked him off, smashing his muzzle against the attacker's ear as he rolled away. The Indian fell back, half-stunned, as Wells jumped to his feet and shot his assailant. Then he staggered toward a nearby wagon for shelter. Halfway there, another Indian jumped on his back and slashed his coat with a knife as Wells whirled away.

Several hours later the nose was taped back on at the field hospital, and in two months it was almost as good as new.

Yellow Bird, who had put the spark to the tinder, raced at the first gunshot to the protection of the two large tents—one in which Mrs. Big Foot had been sitting, the other a headquarters for the scouts. He ducked into the latter and found there Little Bat's prized rifle. He promptly thrust its muzzle through a slit in the tent and began firing at nearby soldiers.

John Shangreau was also running for the tent because his extra ammunition was there. A young lieutenant, frightened and excited, shouted at him, "I guess we've got our revenge for Custer now, eh, Scout?"

Shangreau stopped in his tracks. "You ought to be ashamed, you idiot!" he shot back. "Custer had the guns to protect himself, but here you take the guns away from these people and then massacre them!" Then, disgusted with himself for such babble at a time like this, he dashed ahead toward the tent.

But another soldier yelled at him, "Watch out! Don't go into that tent! There's an Indian in there shooting!"

A young recruit came running forward, calling, "Hold on, I'll get the red bastard out of there!"

Lieutenant Mann, suddenly realizing what the soldier was up to, shrieked, "No, no! Come back!" But it was too late. The soldier slit the side of the tent with his knife, and as he looked in to find his target, Yellow Bird fired point-blank into his stomach. The young man reeled back and his body slumped to the ground.

Mann's troop now turned the tent into a sieve. They also called to the top of the hill for a Hotchkiss shell, which exploded at the tent's side and set it ablaze. Yellow Bird had been dead for several minutes, but the burning tent and hay consumed his clothing and charred his body.

Shangreau meanwhile had returned to the fighting and came across Father Francis Craft, who had been stabbed in the back. The priest had come out with Colonel For-syth to witness the disarming, and despite his severe wound he was moving among the dead and injured.

"Someone did it by mistake in the heavy smoke," he said of the stabbing.

When at last the battle around the former council circle was over, the Indian village lay smoking and barren and the warriors able to do so had all fled. Dust and smoke still hung thick in the air. Philip Wells walked back into the area, now filled with debris and human bodies. A bandage was around his face, holding his nose in place.

He looked down at Iron Eyes' twisted form and said aloud, "Too bad, my friend! I tried to save you but you wouldn't listen."

Then he spoke in a loud voice in the Sioux tongue:

"The white men came to help you people and you have brought death to yourselves. Still, the whites are merciful and they will save the wounded enemy when he is harmless. So if some of you are alive, raise your heads. I am a man of your own blood who says this."

A dozen heads around the bloody field were slowly lifted. Frog raised himself on one elbow. "Are you Fox?" he asked.

This was Wells' name among the Indians, and he said yes.

"Please come near me," said Frog.

Wells was not sure what the man's intention was, and he knelt down cautiously. Frog pointed to Yellow Bird's blackened body and asked, "Who is that burned one?"

"He is the medicine man."

Frog clenched his fist of his free hand and shot it toward the body as he threw his fingers open. This was his curse which said, "I could kill you if it were possible, and even that would not be enough to satisfy me; I only wish I could harm you in some worse way."

Then aloud, for Wells to hear, he said to the dead Yellow Bird, "If I could drag myself over there I would *still* stab you!"

He looked up at Wells' face. "He is our murderer. If he had not incited the young men, we would all be alive and happy."

Wells arose. He saw a slight motion in Mrs. Big Foot's body, but she was plainly close to death.

An Indian nearby now spoke to him: "I am Elks Saw

Him, and I was just visiting Hump's band. I joined up with Big Foot's band by accident because I am an Oglala and wanted to go to Pine Ridge. I had given the soldiers my Winchester willingly, and now I am shot twice."

The scout could think of nothing to say.

Over in the ravine and along Wounded Knee Creek, the cleanup was about finished, so Paddy Starr, a wagon driver, and some scouts went into the ditch and began calling out in Siouan, "All who are alive, raise yourselves up and you will be saved."

The wounded man who had given Dewey Horn Cloud a gun got up painfully from his little hole in the bank and stood up. Two cavalrymen from the cleanup platoon happened at that moment to ride over the edge of the ravine, and they raised their rifles and fired. The old man dropped. A cry of protest arose among the scouts, and the troopers explained that they hadn't heard the call to surrender.

One by one, bleeding and hobbling Indian women now began to climb out of their holes, some of which had been dug with their bare hands.

Captain Godfrey had taken a detachment of cavalry well west of the battle area, shooting down Indians whom they overtook running for the agency and rounding up the herd of Indian ponies which had stampeded during the fighting. They saw some Indians run into the brush of a narrow draw, and pulled up around it.

"*Hau, kola!* Squaw! Papoose!" Godfrey called out two or three times. There was no response.

"All right, fire!" he commanded, and a volley went into the brush. The soldiers walked forward on foot and found a woman and two children writhing as they died. As the men turned to leave, one of them kicked a fourth form lying on its face and he saw the testicles. The body moved suddenly and the soldier put a bullet through the back of its head. Then he turned the body over with his foot and saw a boy, perhaps 10 or 12 years old.

Captain Henry Jackson and Troop C, operating in the same region, trapped eight Minneconjou warriors and twice as many women and children in a gully. A battle began, but shortly some Oglala scouts came up and one of them said he thought some of his relatives were among those in the ditch. So Jackson stopped the firing to let him try negotiation.

After a half hour of loud debate, the Indians agreed to come out if Jackson would pull back his men, which he did. Four Indian men, three of the women and one child had been wounded by the gunfire, and after the rest had filed out of the gully, the soldiers carried the wounded to an ambulance wagon. They were barely done with the job when a band of warriors from Pine Ridge attacked them.

The agency had heard the explosion of shells at Wounded Knee, of course, and one of Forsyth's couriers soon brought word of what was happening. Some of the Indians camped across White Clay Creek began firing into the agency; hundreds of them rode out of town northward to organize for battle or just in plain terror, dragging their families with them. One group, led by Flying Horse, came straight to Wounded Knee to try to help their Minneconjou brothers, and they attacked Jackson's troop with such fury that it was forced to retire to a defense position, leaving the wounded prisoners unguarded in the ambulance.

Flying Horse himself was shot and killed, but the rest of his party rode off westward, taking the ambulance full of wounded with them.

By late afternoon Colonel Forsyth had loaded up his dead and wounded soldiers and as many wounded Indian women and children as could readily be found, and the train started back to Pine Ridge with cavalry ahead and behind. An hour after midnight, the last of the wagons got its sorry contents unloaded at the improvised hospital and undertaking facilities at the agency.

The Indian dead and many wounded had of course been left strewn across the open meadow and along the ravine's bottom where they had fallen or crawled. The next day the winter's first blizzard came at last, and three inches of fine snow was drifted across the frozen and twisted bodies as if attempting to cover the shame of it.

Several hundred Oglala and Brulé warriors started a whole new rebellion as a result of the massacre of their Minneconjou kinsmen at Wounded Knee, and there was desultory fighting for two weeks from the north fork of the Cheyenne to Pine Ridge. Old Red Cloud himself was forced by the "nonprogressives" to flee the agency on the day of the battle, and the evacuation was joined by Big Road, He Dog, Little Wound, Two Strike, No Water and numerous others—all of the old frightened, outraged crowd again. In the next two weeks there were a few military casualties and some shameless murders on both sides.

Kicking Bear and Short Bull had started south from the Stronghold to surrender on December 27, as they had promised. When they were almost about to enter the agency on the twenty-ninth, word came to them of what was happening at Wounded Knee. They immediately turned about, joined by the hundreds of warriors and their families pouring out of Pine Ridge, in anger and terror.

But during the next few days the chiefs of these bands were wrangling constantly, and General Miles had them surrounded by 3,500 men—nearly half of all the infantry and cavalry of the United States Army. Gradually, avoiding contact as much as possible, the military jostled the rebels back toward the agency a few miles at a time. And on January 15, 1891, their spirits broken by daily defections, the rebellious warriors paraded in two columns up White Clay Creek to within sight of the agency—4,000 Indians riding or driving some 7,000 horses, at least 500 wagons, and half as many travois. Their camp that night ran for three miles along both sides of the creek.

Big Road sent word to General Brooke that he was collecting the Indians' rifles. He wanted no repetition of Wounded Knee. He turned in 200 stand of arms, and although Miles knew there were five times as many Indian guns around, he now judiciously ignored the matter.

The day after Wounded Knee's tragedy, Paddy Starr, the freighter, was given the contract to go back out and bury the dead Indians at two dollars a body. The snowstorm continued for two days, so the burial party did not go to Wounded Knee until January first. Then a detail of soldiers and a considerable crowd of Indians went along, most of the latter looking for missing relatives. Dr. Charles A. Eastman, the agency physician and a fullblooded Santee Sioux, accompanied the work crew.

Starr's men camped that night in and around Mousseau's store and finished their work the next day. They dug a long trench on top of the hill where the Hotchkiss guns had stood. The ground was frozen hard and it took much digging. Then they picked up the frozen bodies around the battlefield and piled them into wagons, hauling them up the hill and dumping them in the open grave. Some of the corpses did not give up easily, because they were frozen to the dry grass with their own blood.

The workmen and soldiers stripped many souvenirs from the bodies before burying them, and the grave contained three layers of corpses when finally the work was finished and the trench was refilled with earth. Starr claimed that he had buried 168 bodies. Nobody knew who most of them were, but one of the crew took note that Chief Big Foot's body was the fourth one dropped into the trench. When the haulers had come to him there on the field in his government-issue greatcoat and his huge shoes, the freezing process had distorted his large frame into a grotesque shape. His elbows were braced on the ground and his head and shoulders were raised slightly as if he were trying, even in death, to maintain the dignity and responsibility of his chieftainship. His hands were lifted in a faintly esthetic gesture, and one eye remained open, still watching over the dead brood scattered across the battlefield. The white cloth band which had been used to relieve his final suffering was, at the end, tied around his head as a scarf.

The charnel wagon pulled up alongside the twisted form and a teamster called out, "Hey! Look who I got! Somebody get aholt and help me lift this big ox." It finally took three men to toss the frozen hulk on the pile in the wagon.

Three women who were interred had plainly been pregnant. One 10-year-old boy's arm and shoulder had been shot away by the Hotchkiss shell which hit a fleeing wagon, and near his body lay the mother of Shoots-With-Hawk's-Feather without sign of an abdomen.

William Peano, a French-Indian member of the crew,

counted among the buried 24 old men whom he judged to be noncombatants, six small boys, seven babies in their cradleboards, seven old women, and 102 able-bodied boys and girls, men and women, from the age of ten upward. This made 146 corpses, and Peano always contended his figure was accurate despite Starr's claim of 168.

The burial party then returned to the agency, considering its work done, but a good many dead and wounded were found during the next two weeks by search parties, both white and Indian. Seven wounded men and women were found along Wounded Knee Creek, alive despite the bitter storm. Others were found in vacant cabins and sheds in the vicinity to which they had crawled. One blind old woman had lain under a wagon through the blizzard for three nights without food or water, but was alive when Dr. Eastman discovered her.

Frank Feather, an agency policeman, and other searchers in the burial party found three live babies. Young Bull Bear and his wife on Medicine Root Creek took one of them, Charging Bear on Pass Creek another. Captain George E. Bartlett of the agency police heard one of the infants crying under a pile of dead women in a hole where they had crawled, and the child lived to maturity.

As least seven of the 51 wounded Indians hauled to Pine Ridge the night of the battle, and unloaded at the Episcopal Mission there, died of their wounds within a day or two. The total of Indian dead who could be accounted for during the following week was 184, but unquestionably some of the wounded carried away by the Indians had died elsewhere.

The number of whites killed was 25—Captain Wallace, six noncommissioned officers and 18 privates. Thirty-seven soldiers had been wounded—and the two civilians, Philip Wells and Father Craft.

Some years later, surviving Indian relatives erected a monument at the mass grave which says, among other things, "Many innocent women and children who knew no wrong died here."

One can hardly argue with that.

EPILOG

On the day before the surrender, as Big Foot's people were nearing Medicine Root Creek, a squad of Oglala scouts some miles to the east, under the command of Standing Soldier, came across 73 Hunkpapa refugees from Standing Rock Reservation. A span of oxen was hauling their luggage in a wagon, and they had 31 head of horses.

Standing Soldier and his 15 men had been out for two days looking for Big Foot's band, but the Minneconjous had passed to the west of them. Now the Oglala scouts had a different problem.

The 38 Hunkpapas who, in order to avoid arrest by Colonel Sumner, had slipped away from Big Foot's village on Deep Creek the night before the Minneconjou flight, had drifted eastward and stumbled across a similar group of their neighbors from Grand River who also had been running ever since the Sitting Bull fight. Discovering Colonel Merriam ahead of them on the Cheyenne, the two groups decided to try to get to the Stronghold and join the ghost dancers, so they turned southwest. But here they almost fell into the hands of Colonel Carr's troops, so they bent wide to the southeast again. Without knowing it, they had almost overtaken the now plodding Minneconjou caravan when Standing Soldier and his scouts came upon them.

Fortunately for Standing Soldier, he had among his men a Hunkpapa, Crazy Thunder, who had spent the years in Canada with Sitting Bull's people, but afterward had gone to live at Pine Ridge. Some of the Standing Rock Indians recognized him and there was a warm reunion among them, Crazy Thunder shaking hands all around and greeting old friends.

With this good start, Standing Soldier the diplomatist spoke to the Hunkpapa warriors with great sympathy for their plight. He had seen two or three stray cattle at Black Prairie Chicken's abandoned ranch nearby, and he ordered them killed to provide a hearty meal, after which the Oglala scouts shared all of their remaining tobacco with the Hunkpapas.

When everyone was fed and relaxed, Standing Soldier asked them to hear him.

"Most of the people at the Stronghold have gone to the agency," he said. "They are being well treated and well fed. You would be wise to come there with me. I assure you that you will be welcomed and cared for."

The Hunkpapas were tired and poorly clothed. Assured by Crazy Thunder that his leader spoke the truth, they soon agreed to follow him.

The next day, as these parties were moving southwest, they came upon the fresh trail of Big Foot's band. Immediately Standing Soldier sent one of his men, Last Horse, ahead with two other scouts to overtake the Minneconjous and tell them to wait, so that the whole group could go together into Pine Ridge. Standing Soldier made camp that night on American Horse Creek, near where Big Foot's people had camped only the night before.

They were hardly started on the trail the following morning when they heard the rumble of gunfire and cannon ahead. Standing Soldier told his Hunkpapas not to worry—that soldiers regularly saluted their officers with gunfire in this manner. But suspecting the truth, he slowed down, and early in the afternoon Last Horse returned to tell of the horror at Wounded Knee.

"The air still stinks of gunpowder," he said. "I have orders for you to disarm these Hunkpapas and break up their guns!"

Standing Soldier was much too wise to attempt anything of that kind. Instead, he sent Last Horse to Pine Ridge to notify General Brooke that he was bringing in the wandering Hunkpapas. Then, without a word to explain the detour, he led the refugees straight south around Porcupine Creek, made an arc 10 or 12 miles below Wounded Knee, and after camping one more night, paraded into Pine Ridge in a snowstorm on December 30.

Three miles from the agency, Standing Soldier stopped the march and made a brief speech to his prisoners:

"The Great Father has told us in our treaties to live in peace with the white man. That is why we Oglalas have gone to so much trouble to protect you Hunkpapa brothers and bring you safely to the agency. Now I ask you to show your goodwill by handing your guns over to the womenfolk for safekeeping, and by doing whatever the soldiers tell you to do when we arrive."

So the warriors marched in without a gun in their hands. That is the way that Standing Soldier, an Indian scout, dealt with the problem.

When they found General Brooke, the Hunkpapas said they would give him their guns and do whatever he wished. They camped near White Clay Creek, and have lived among the Oglalas ever since.

ACKNOWLEDGMENTS

The objective of this research into the Wounded Knee story was to better understand, if possible, the personality and behavior of Chief Big Foot and certain other principals, with neither maudlin sentiment about the Indian, racial prejudice, or military chauvinism. This dimension would still be largely speculation if it were not for the exhaustive reminiscences of so many participants in the Wounded Knee affair, contained in the Eli S. Ricker Collection of manuscripts at the Nebraska State Historical Society in Lincoln. Otherwise there is little in the way of a written record about Big Foot except for the United States Army reports and other official documents, including those in the Bureau of Indian Affairs, and these even at their best have a bias, naturally, that seldom did justice to the Teton Dakota point of view.

After a career as county judge and newspaper editor in northwest Nebraska, Ricker began, about 1905, a remarkable series of interviews with Indians, cowboys, scouts, soldiers—anyone who had been involved in any way in the conflicts between the Dakota or Sioux federation and the white man. He filled literally scores of notebooks and tablets with the recollections of these persons, scribbled mostly in longhand, in addition to hundreds of personal letters, newspaper clippings and other source material. Especially rich in anecdote and recollection regarding the Big Foot story are the interviews with Philip P. Wells, Dewey Beard (formerly Horn Cloud), Joseph Horn Cloud, and John Shangreau, while his talks with William Peano, Standing Soldier, Frank Feather, Richard C. Stirk and many others offering interesting and important details.

190

This firsthand record sometimes puts a quite different face than that shown by the military reports on much that happened before and after Wounded Knee, and permits us to make more knowledgeable deductions about motives and intentions at many points. I am indebted to Donald D. Snoddy, assistant archivist of the Nebraska State Historical Society, for his assistance and helpful counsel during my search through the Ricker material.

The matter dealing with Wovoka, the Paiute messiah, comes almost exclusively from the classic work of James Mooney, "The Ghost Dance Religion and the Sioux Outbreak of 1890," published with the 14th Annual Report of the Bureau of American Ethnology, 1892-3, Part II, although James P. Boyd used some of the same material in his "Recent Indian Wars" (Publishers Union, Philadelphia, 1891). Boyd also provided much of the comment about the Sioux uprising by General Nelson A. Miles and other contemporary personalities.

Certainly the most scholarly and comprehensive of the historical treatments of the events of 1890-91 on the Sioux reservations is Robert M. Utley's "The Last Days of the Sioux Nation" (Yale University Press, 1963), although Doane Robinson's earlier "History of the Dakota or Sioux Indians" (South Dakota Historical Collections, Vol. II, 1904; reprinted, Ross and Haines, Minneapolis, 1967) is invaluable. Also, James H. McGregor gathered vital material in helping to mark the fiftieth anniversary of Wounded Knee and in renewing the long-futile plea for restitution to the victims with his book, "The Wounded Knee Massacre From the Viewpoint of the Survivors" (Lund Press, Minneapolis, 1940).

Of course the "official" sources for the Wounded Knee tragedy and much that went before it are, primarily, the annual reports of the Secretary of War for these years and of the Commissioner of Indian Affairs, Department of the Interior. And it would be unfair not to mention the personal story of that "old pro" among Indian agents, James McLaughlin, "My Friend the Indian" (Houghton Mifflin Co., Boston, 1910). The gospel according to Kicking Bear which I have quoted is from this entertaining book, and I trust Mr. McLaughlin's spirit will forgive me for having it delivered at Little Wound's camp instead of Sitting Bull's—but I assume that Kicking Bear made the same speech everywhere he went.

For certain other comments and story details I am indebted to Stanley Vestal's "New Sources of Indian History, 1850-91" (University of Oklahoma Press, 1934) and his "Sitting Bull, Champion of the Sioux" (University of Oklahoma Press, 1957).

Words can hardly tell how much gracious assistance was provided to me by the staff of the American Antiquarian Society at Worcester, Massachusetts, and by Janice Fleming, Librarian of the South Dakota State Historical Society, now the Historical Research Center of the State Department of Education and Cultural Affairs, at Pierre. Similarly, generous help of numerous kinds was given me by John Popowski, then Director of the South Dakota Department of Game, Fish and Parks—not the least of which was an adequate understanding of the almost inaccessible terrain around the Stronghold region in the Bad Lands, which I had been able to view only from Cuny Table and Sheep Mountain Table nearby.

Mrs. Naomi Broken Rope responded graciously to my request for some help with translation of the Sioux tongue, and John Milton, editor of The South Dakota Review, gave me sound advice in the same area. In addition to all those named above, my principal sources were:

Ralph K. Andrist, "The Long Death; The Last Days of

the Plains Indians" (The Macmillan Co., New York, 1964).

Paul Bailey, "Ghost Dance Messiah" (Westerlore Press, Los Angeles, 1970).

John G. Bourke, "On the Border With Crook" (University of Nebraska Press, 1971; originally published 1891).

Dee Brown, "Bury My Heart at Wounded Knee" (Holt, Rinehart & Winston, New York, 1970).

Charles A. Eastman, "From the Deep Woods to Civilization" (Little, Brown & Co., Boston, 1916); also "Indian Boyhood" (McClure, Phillips & Co., New York, 1902).

John F. Finerty, "War-path and Bivouac; the Big Horn and Yellowstone Expedition" (Lakeside Press, Chicago, 1955; originally published 1890).

Grant Foreman, "The Last Trek of the Indians" (University of Chicago Press, 1946).

Henry E. Fritz, "The Movement for Indian Assimilation, 1860-90" (University of Pennsylvania Press, Philadelphia, 1963).

"Handbook of American Indians" (U.S. Bureau of Ethnology, Bulletin No. 30, 1907).

Stan Hoig, "The Sand Creek Massacre" (University of Oklahoma Press, Norman, 1961).

George E. Hyde, "A Sioux Chronicle" (University of Oklahoma Press, 1956).

William Fitch Kelley, "Pine Ridge 1890," edited and compiled by Alexander Kelley and Pierre Bovis (Pierre Bovis, San Francisco, 1971).

Garrick Mallery, "Picture-Writing of the American Indians" (Dover Publications, New York, 1972; originally published with the Tenth Annual Report, U.S. Bureau of Ethnology, 1888-89, Washington, 1893).

Gordon MacGregor, "Warriors Without Weapons" (University of Chicago Press, 1946).

Marshall Sprague, "Massacre; the Tragedy at White River" (Little, Brown & Co., Boston, 1957).

John R. Swanton, "The Indian Tribes of North America" (Smithsonian Institution Press, Washington, 1952).

J. W. Vaughn, "Indian Fights; New Facts on Seven Encounters" (University of Oklahoma Press, 1966); also "With Crook at the Rosebud" (Stackpole Press, Harrisburg, 1956).

Stanley Vestal, "Warpath and Council Fire" (Houghton, Mifflin Co., Boston, 1934).

Clark Wissler, "The American Indian" (Oxford University Press, New York, 1938; also "North American Indians of the Plains" (American Museum of Natural History, New York, 1948).